Bigfoot and Woolybooger Tales 2

Bigfoot and Woolybooger Tales 2

Compiled and Edited by Judith Victoria Hensley

Kindle Direct Publishing

ISBN: 9798560776312
Imprint: Independently Published

Cover Design: Lakeview Times

Printed by Kindle Direct Publishing, an Amazon.com Company

Dedication

For Alex and Maren,
Ethan and Ella,
Jeremy and Jenn

Thank You

To everyone who shared a story and images for this collection

Wikipedia CCO Public Domain Image Used as A Story Marker for each entry.

Disclaimer

Each story recorded on these pages are the intellectual property of the individual story tellers. The truth of each story lays with the individuals who shared them and is not questioned by, or the responsibility to validate of the editor. This collection of stories is not an effort to prove a scientific fact or establish a new species. Each book in the *Bigfoot and Woolybooger Tale Series* is meant to be a safe place for others to share what they have seen and heard with those who have had similar encounters, love a good story, or who have a genuine interest in the subject matter.

Stories included in the *Bigfoot and Woolybooger Tales Series*, and this book, Bigfoot and Woolybooger Tales2 are not the express opinion of the editor. They are stories recorded for the sake of preservation.

Bigfoot and Woolybooger Tales, the first collection, is available on Amazon and Kindle.

Bigfoot and Woolybooger Tales 2 is also available there.

At this time, there is no plan for a new collection, but depending on public response, this could change.

To share a story: judith99@bellsouth
          OR on Facebook contact Judith Victoria Hensley

These books may also be of interest:
Panther Tales
Panther Tales 2
Panther Tales 3

Message from the Editor

The birth of this project is an interesting one. Having seen black panther cats on several occasions and having been scoffed at and laughed at by officials, I set out to find other stories from people with sightings. For over forty years since I saw the first big black cat, I've been asking people and listening to their stories on the subject.

At some point I felt that it wasn't enough for me to hear them and forget them over time. This may have validated my own sightings, but they were more important than that. They needed to be documented in printed form for others to share. I have currently published three volumes of *Panther Tales* (available on Amazon and Kindle). In the process of gathering stories for those books, another set of stories emerged.

People who spent a great deal of time in the woods and have seen black panther, mountain lions, and/or bobcats are also people who may have seen a creature that is known by the names of bigfoot, sasquatch, booger, or many others for the same creature. I wasn't interested in the whole bigfoot movement and didn't realize how big it has become across the country and around the world until I started listening to the stories people were telling me.

I had seen the Patterson-Gimlin footage from the 1960s and believed it to be very real or an excellent hoax. I didn't feel qualified to make the call.

Either way, I found it fascinating to consider the possibility that such a primate is alive and well on this planet. New species are identified every year.

My personal belief is that God loves diversity in the plant and animal world. The Bible records Him as "Creator."

The account of creation says that on the seventh day, God rested. It does not say that he stopped creating. I have no quarrel with the process of evolution in the hands of God who set it all in motion with his master plan. Why couldn't there be black panther? Why couldn't there be bigfoot?

I love a good story well told about many topics. I love to listen to the rhythm and flow of language as people talk. I love the lyrical melody of spoken words in local dialects and accents. I love the poetic language of similes and metaphors that has prevailed in Appalachia and surrounding areas over generations and is still common in the speech of older individuals in the area. Listening to and recording stories audibly or in print is a great joy to me.

Hearing so many stories about woolyboogers or unidentified creatures, it seemed to become a responsibility to save them in some form before they're lost forever. I regret the ones I've heard over the years and don't recall and can't revisit them because they weren't saved.

I have never seen a sasquatch. I don't want to.

I have had unexplained things happen to me in the woods when I was younger, like pebbles being thrown lightly at me, which made no sense at the time. As soon as I'd try to turn around and catch whoever was tossing them, they would stop, and I'd see no one. As soon as I'd start hiking again, they'd start again.

I finally explained it away in my mind as squirrels, knowing full well that squirrels don't toss pebbles.

I've seen structures in the woods that looked like they were deliberately formed but held no meaning for me other than a moment of curiosity about who built them and why. I've seen structures very similar to the ones contained in this book and the ones that seemed to form a teepee with an opening on one side. I wrote it off to children playing in the woods.

On one occasion I even found a large footprint in a light spring snow with green grass showing through and wondered why in the world anyone would be walking barefoot in the snow that time of year. I chalked the huge print up to teenagers wading the creek for some unknown reason and trying to keep their shoes dry.

I know the smell of bear, skunk, horses, and wet dog. I have smelled on several occasions the red-hot smell of stink that would almost blow a person over. One whiff in my nose was enough to alert me that something out of the ordinary was near. I have written those times off as a very stinky bear that had just done its business in the woods. One recurrence was so often we referred to the stink as coming from "Vomit Bear."

During one unexplained incident I was with several other individuals walking at night down a country road. We knew something was following us in the field beside of the road. It was walking parallel and keeping pace with us. We thought it was a dog or a deer. When we got to the end of the pasture, there was a bridge that crossed a creek running around behind the field. Something let out a sound that scared us all to death. The volume and nearness of it was overwhelming. It was a howling/growling/yowling kind of roar that I hope I never hear again.

I didn't attach any real significance to any of those incidents at the times they occurred. I knew nothing of woolyboogers, bigfoot, or sasquatch, except as a means to scare children.

Until the stories of bigfoot/sasquatch/ and woolyboogers began to surface while I was collecting panther tales, I just didn't connect the dots.

I also became a huge fan of *Finding Bigfoot* on the Discovery Channel and tried never to miss an episode. My favorite part of each show was the town hall meetings when people who had experienced sightings or had encounters with sasquatch showed up to tell their stories to the cast and crew of *Finding Bigfoot*. The TV show's team members traveled across the country searching for eyewitnesses and evidence.

I don't want to see a Woolybooger. I don't want to interact with a sasquatch. I'm content with hearing stories without ever coming face to face with a bigfoot. Even if I knew where I could go and photograph one in the wild, I don't think I'd want the responsibility of knowing that they truly exist and having irrefutable proof in my hands. If I had the experience, it would surely be something I couldn't keep to myself.

What I have learned through listening to all the stories included in this book and the last collection of *Bigfoot and Woolybooger Tales* is that the story tellers are people of integrity, intelligence, and sincerity who are telling the truth about their experiences. I can't say they've all seen bigfoot for certain, but I can say without a doubt that they've seen something I haven't.

These encounters are very real to them and I ask all readers to consider them with sincere objectivity and be respectful to man and beast as opinions are formed.

Table of Contents

Original Artwork by Paul Nolan

Other Names for Bigfoot
Collected from websites, blogs, research, and oral traditions from the region

Woodwose

Wudewasa

Wildman

Almas

Almasty

Grey Man

Grogoch

Skookum

Evil Man of the Woods

Cuatlacas

Menk

Guardian of the Woods

Wood Guardian

Forest People

Hairy Man

Yeti

Wooly booger

Tree People

Wood Booger

Skunk Ape

Fouke Monster

Old Wise One

Grandfather of the Forest

Nimbjim

Ape Monkey

Sasquatch

Saracen

Genoskwa

Kushtuka

Monkey Bear
Squatch
Squal Man
Yeti
Wild Man
Oma
Strendoo
Yowie
Yerren
Man bear
Nephilim
Devil Monkey
Gerendel
Kakundak
Windego
Phantom of the Forest
Momo
Wachuk
Wood ape
Wompas

Public Domain Image

Connections Between Bigfoot and Black Panthers
Cliff Barackman
(North American Bigfoot Center and Museum)
Former Co-Host of *Finding Bigfoot*

Any large animals (which would certainly include bigfoot and black panthers on the large end of the spectrum) need food, water, and cover. Anywhere those things are abundant, I think it can be expected to find the other large animals as well.

I've compared sasquatch behavior and diet to that of a black bear. Bears are very large omnivores. There are also predatory similarities between sasquatch and mountain lions. They may hunt slightly differently in some ways, but they are both going after the deer, rabbits, opossums, raccoons, and all the other meat packets walking around in the woods. I think these species overlap not only in habitat, but also in some behaviors as well.

We tend to think at this point that sasquatch are ambush predators with some cooperative hunting as well. I don't think they fit very neatly into one category versus others. I believe they overlap in a lot of ways, behaviors especially.

There are plenty of game cam pictures of mountain lions perched up on top of rocks surveying their terrain. I think sasquatch do the same thing for the same reasons. They look for deer herds to follow, hoping they can spot a straggler.

These large animals have the same needs. They're going after deer, rabbit, and whatever else they can catch. They're very secretive animals, largely nocturnal, slinky, and Ninja-like as they walk around in the woods remaining undetected. I think a lot of this behavior overlaps with big cats and sasquatches.

As far as researching sasquatch, I've kind of taken the Hippocratic oath, to do no harm to the subject, to the credibility of the subject, bigfoot, or anybody associated with these animals. I'm striving to make sure that if I keep it real, always tell the truth, and move forward, and to make sure that the subject is being taken seriously, that's my goal. I don't want to do anything to bring mockery or scoffers to this thing that I love. That's where my heart is.

Sometimes people misinterpret cougar screams for sasquatch screams. They are similar in some ways, but people are usually mistaken in what they're hearing if it sounds like a scream.

During the Town Hall Meetings we held for *Finding Bigfoot* episodes, we heard a lot, A LOT, TONS of mountain lion and black panther stories, along with the bigfoot stories. The mountain lion and black panther stories didn't make the edit, of course. They didn't end up on the screen because our work concentrated only on sasquatch stories and encounters.

In my opinion, the reason the Department of Wildlife, the state and federal agencies don't recognize that panthers or mountain lions live in certain places, like Pennsylvania, is all monetary. If they do recognize officially that there are mountain lions or black panthers living in a state instead of only passing through, then they must develop some sort of a plan for them. This would cost hundreds of thousands of dollars, if not more.

It's all monetary. There is an incentive in keeping sasquatch and these things in the realm of mythology. Consider all the damage the snail darter fishes, or the spotted owl did back in the 1990s. That whole thing shut down the logging industry in a lot of places and in those places it still hasn't recovered. Having a sasquatch, or even a mountain lion in a place where they're not supposed to be recognized would cause a lot of trouble.

Politicians, being what they are, serve a different master than the rest of us. They serve the economy. They serve the dollar bill, which is their central focus. Of course, they don't want to have to deal with the presence of an unknown or endangered species that would interrupt commerce. From their perspective, serving the almighty dollar as their interpretation of serving the people, what is the most cost-effective way of dealing with something like the presence of sasquatch?

The most cost-effective way to deal with this problem if it should come, is to not do anything at all. The presence of these species is being taken care of for free. They're naturally elusive, hard to find, and rare to see. So, if there's not solid documentation of their existence, nothing must be done. No money must be spent to try and protect them.

The people who go paranormal with it, that sasquatches are UFO riding, interdimensional, shape shifting entities, or "whatever they are," are the people who end up on the news. They give the rest of the researchers a bad name. They misrepresent the subject, in my opinion.

Who would take the rest of us seriously with these people out there claiming what they claim?

So, officials, departments, and politicians do have it under control from a cost perspective. Unfortunately, they're missing the boat about what we could learn from these creatures and how we might benefit from them. It's all about the money they don't have to spend if they don't acknowledge these rare creatures. These places and departments are underfunded already. Where would the money come from to protect them? They'd have to divert funds

The wild lands and the animals that be are not a high priority to those making decisions about them because they don't turn a profit. It's part of the whole problem. Instead of capitalism being a tool of the people, people have become tools of capitalism. Officials serve that ideology instead of serving the people. That's a real problem.

The animals are the same. THEY are the meek that shall inherit the earth. They're the ones with no voice. So, people who care about such things and research these animals are the ones who must watch out for their right to exist.

As far as areas of concentration of sasquatch in the United States, wherever a small group of sasquatches are, they're seen enough that people know they're there. I wouldn't say that California, although famous for bigfoot sightings, is necessarily a hot spot. The state is so big! I think it's easier to find sasquatches on the east coast because there are less huge tracts of forest.

In Pennsylvania, for example, there's an area that's about a three mile by seven-mile patch of woods connected with other three mile by seven-mile patches of woods by tendrils of green belts. Those are the easier spots to find sasquatches because there are smaller habitats to look at.

In Oregon where I live, everywhere is good habitat for sasquatches. So, how do you begin to narrow it down? There are ways to do it, but smaller habitat is easier to study. A lot of stories are coming out of the Daniel Boone National Forest.

In the last five years one of the best places that has more evidence, more sighting reports, and all that is northern Kentucky, in Trimble County specifically. There are a group of sasquatches living there. The most important thing, the key part that really sets all that aside is that there's an investigator there whose very active. Where bigfoots are hanging out and people are seeing them, but there's no investigator around, and no one is talking about it, we don't get to hear about that stuff.

A lot of it comes down to who is around that is interested. Who can you tell if you see or have an encounter with a sasquatch? The guy in Trimble County, Tom Shay, is retired and he's on his local Facebook a lot. People tell him about bigfoot sightings. When he hears about an incident, he will go to that place and investigate if possible. A lot of times he comes back with footprint casts. He's gathered more evidence than anybody I know. That's for sure. He's a good solid guy who's not easily fooled and his heart's in the right place.

Right now, I think northern Kentucky is about as good a place for sasquatch as you can get anywhere. For more information go to:

Northern Kentucky Bigfoot Research Group

Bigfootlore.blogspot.com

* * *

Addendum from the editor of this book in case any of the readers are not familiar with the television series **Finding Bigfoot**:

Finding Bigfoot was an American television series on Animal Planet which can still be seen through public media. It premiered on May 29, 2011. The program followed four researchers and explorers while they investigated potential evidence of Bigfoot, a cryptid hominid allegedly living in the wildernesses of the United States and Canada. While the *Finding Bigfoot* team never captured photographic evidence of the creature's existence, the show gained high ratings and was a top earner for Animal Planet. The series finale and the 100th episode was released on May 27, 2018

The team consisted of Bigfoot Field Researchers Organization (BFRO) founder and President Matt Moneymaker, researchers James "Bobo" Fay and Cliff Barackman, and skeptical scientist Ranae Holland. The series never questioned the existence of bigfoot, but rather documented the team's search efforts and study of potential evidence to prove the existence of the creature.

Cliff Barackman was born and raised in Long Beach, California, Barackman currently resides in Portland, Oregon. The evidence analyst of the group has been a dedicated sasquatch field researcher for the past two decades. He has been known to spend over 200 days a year in the field. He is also an accomplished jazz guitarist holding a Bachelor of Arts degree from California State University, Long Beach.

Public Daomain Image – August 1895112

The Unexpected Encounters that Shaped My Life
Michael Cook (Cook Cryptid Research)

October 8, 2018 was a beautiful day. It was cool enough to wear jackets without getting too warm. Gwendolynn Guthrie, Kenny Howard Smith, and I went for a hike to a place I chose. Glen Mink, a bigfoot researcher friend, and I had a double sighting of sasquatch back in 2016 in the area around the same time of the year. After having heard about the story, Kenny and Gwen wanted to go with me to see where the incident had taken place.

We climbed up the Berea Pinnacles, which is just outside of Berea, Kentucky. It's about a mile and a half hike straight up the side of a mountain. Once at the top of the lookout, a person realizes it may have been hard to get there, but it's worth it.

On a clear day, it's possible to see the Fifth-Third building in Lexington from there. The view is amazing in all directions. It was a great day.

Staying after dark was nowhere in my plan. When we packed up for the day I had said, "We don't need to take flashlights because we're not going to be there after dark."

Time flew past while we enjoyed the surrounding scenery on top of the point. Someone commented about the beautiful sunset and it dawned on me that if we'd stayed until the sun was setting from up there, it was going to be getting dark quickly in the woods.

"We've got to get off this mountain," I said. "If we let it get dark on us, we'll never be able to see well enough to find our way out."

The only lights we had with us were the ones on our cell phones. Kenny came to the rescue with three small keychain flashlights that were about an inch or two long. They were dim, but nevertheless, something to see by.

We made our way off the mountain and were half-way down what's referred to as "the bad part." It's literally a rock face almost straight up and down. I was helping Gwen down and Kenny was coming down on his own, near us.

I heard a noise on the ridge that sounded like something scooting. I kept listening and the sound was odd. Not everything that moves in the forest is bigfoot and I know that, but the noise didn't sound like anything I'd ever heard before.

We all got down that rough spot and I told Gwen, "We need to hurry."

What I was thinking to myself was, "*If we have to run, we can't run downhill without someone getting hurt. That's a good way for one of us to fall and kill ourselves!*"

Kenny and Gwen were walking in front of me. I was bringing up the rear and listening intently. I could hear something moving, as if it were following us down the hill. Then Kenny heard it.

He was adamant when he asked, "Did you hear that?"

I said, "No, man… What?... Keep moving. We'll stop and listen when we got on down and out of here." I didn't tell him I'd heard something because I didn't want them to start freaking out before we got back to the cars.

We continued to walk as fast as we could in the dark, using our little flashlights. We came to a little dip that was flat. It was a couple of hundred yards away from our cars. I decided it was time to tell them the truth.

"Listen, y'all. We've been followed the whole way out. I heard it way back up on the trail. I can try to communicate with them, but chances are, if it's a bigfoot, they're not going to do a thing to us. They're pretty shy creatures, but they're curious."

I picked up a small tree limb on the ground and hit a nearby tree one time, known in bigfoot research as a wood knock. When I hit the tree, just on the ridge above us was a tree knock returned.

I looked at Gwen and said, "Start filming."

We had all had trouble with our phones after we started our hike but marked it up to poor reception. My phone was dead. When we started into the woods, my phone was on full charge.

As soon as we got in the woods, though, my phone was drained of power. Kenny's was the same way. The lights kept flickering off and on.

There was some kind of energy disturbance around us, for sure.

Gwen pulled out her phone and started filming. She had charged her phone up with a portable power cell on top of the mountain. Her phone still had a good charge. While she was getting it turned on and set to film, I heard a noise on one ridge, and then a noise on another ridge.

She started filming and on the video, I was recorded, saying, "At this moment, I know of at least two creatures that are around us." Her phone went off, even though she had charged it not long before.

She said, "I've got a way to do this. I'm going YouTube Live." In that mode, whatever you're filming gets saved automatically. So, she got on her YouTube Channel and went live. By then it was late at night and nobody was watching, but her phone was recording.

After that, everything went a little crazy. We heard what sounded like stomping around us. At one time I heard six different movements. Now, dd that mean there were six different bigfoots around us? No, it did not. If just means I heard six different movements, period.

One could have thrown something while it was walking, and I would have heard it walking in one spot and whatever it threw landing in another at the same time. So, I figure there were between four and six beings around us at one time.

Gwen has a long pedigree of Native American family heritage. Her grandmother was full blooded Native American. So, Gwen knew a lot of the Native American wisdom, folklore, and so on.

She drew a large circle in the dirt with other marks in it. It was the symbol for protection. If a person draws this symbol on the ground and stays in it, they will be protected. If they step out of the circle, they are not protected. I don't claim to know everything about that, so I'm going to leave that part right there.

Gwen stood in the middle of this circle drawing and crouched down.

Kenny went from, "Cool! This is exciting!" to "Man, we've got to get out of here!"

The more I watched Kenny, the more I was concerned with what was going on. I had two people that I cared about deeply and had put them in imminent danger. I thought, *"If something happens to one of them, it's on me."*

I walked over to Kenny and put my hand on his chest and patted him. I could feel his heartbeat through his shirt. He was cold and clammy.

I said, "Kenny, are you okay, Buddy?"

He said, "No! I have heart issues."

I said, "Well if you didn't, you do now. Let's get on out of here. We've pushed our luck."

Gwen was about ten feet away from us, still crouched down in her circle. I'm thinking to myself, *"Alright. I've got to get us out of here."*

By then, we could all feel the presence of these creatures and a sense of danger. I pulled my pistol out of my backpack and put it in my belt clip. I didn't figure I'd need it. In October there are no snakes or anything to worry about, so I had carried it in the backpack.

The pistol was there just in case of an animal attack. It wasn't there for bigfoot. I'm not a killer kind of guy. I don't like that people think there's going to have to be a body in order to prove bigfoot exists. I really don't like that.

I walked up to Gwen, reached out my hand and touched her. "Hey, Babe. We've got to go. Kenny's freaking out and we need to get out of here."

As soon as I put my hand on her shoulder, something ran straight toward me. Somehow, although I do not remember doing it (and Gwen will tell you the same thing), I drew my firearm. When I looked down, Gwen was up underneath my hip behind me and I had my firearm pointed at the movement.

"Don't come any closer!" I said. "I don't know if you understand me. I don't know if you can hear me. I don't know, but don't come any closer. Let us leave!" I was screaming into the darkness. "All we want to do is leave. We're not bothering you, so don't hurt us!"

I looked at Gwen and said, "You and Kenny go on. Go ahead of me."

She said, "What about you?"

I said, "I'm good. I'm okay. If something happens, run! But don't run unless something happens. Get to the car and call 911, but don't even utter the word bigfoot. If you do, they won't come."

She said again, "What about you?" I said, "I'm fine. I'm perfectly okay with this."

Cliff Barackman's famous words from Animal Planet's *Finding Bigfoot,* were, "If I had to choose my way to die, it would be to be ripped apart by a bigfoot."

Trust me when I say, I am NOT the same way. I want to go in my sleep, peacefully, just like my grandpa. I was at peace with God and the universe. I had no fear of dying. I'm a researcher and I'm curious about what's on the other side of this life. Is it truly streets of gold, or a mountaintop?

It seemed like I might be getting ready to find out!

We headed toward the cars with Gwen and Kenny ahead of me. I looked at my phone again. I'm thinking, *"Let's try it."*

I pushed the power button and got phone signal, battery life of about one percent. That was enough for a short phone call or a text. The only one I could think about at that moment was my kid, my son Peyton. I sent him a message. "Hey, Bub! I'm thinking about you and I love you."

If something did happen to me, if it were going to be my end, probably nobody would ever know what truly happened to me. They'd think Gwen and Kenny were crazy if they tried to convince someone that I was abducted or murdered by bigfoot. They'd be likely to end up in a home somewhere if they told what happened. (My imagination was going.)

I thought to myself, *"No matter what happens to me, Gwen and Kenny will be safe. I'm the one who put them in imminent danger. If anybody must go tonight, it should be me."*

They continued to walk in front of me. I pulled my firearm out and made sure it was loaded. In my head I directed my thoughts to the creatures. I said, *"I don't know if you can hear me."* Obviously, they didn't hear me when I was screaming at them, so I tried a different approach.

I had heard of people who believe sasquatches have the ability to communicate telepathically. *"If you come close to any of us, I'm unloading my weapon. One way or the other this gun will be unloaded by the time you get done with me. I'm done. Do I want that to happen? No. But I'm telling you right now that I'm not scared."*

Whether they could hear my thoughts or not, who knows.

I walked on down the trail behind Gwen and Kenny, who were about ten to fifteen feet ahead of me. I took out my little flashlight and shined it over my shoulder, looking behind me. If something is going to get me, I want to see it coming. I didn't want to be surprised.

The trail was about eight feet wide. A tall, large silhouette, without details, took one step to cross an eight-foot path. I didn't see any facial features or hair, no details except the size and shape. It was maybe five yards behind me when it stepped across the trail.

No more logical, calm, thinking through things at that point. I got the getty-up-and go! I caught up with Kenny and Gwen and put a hand on each of their backs. "Go! Go! Go! Go! Go!"

I had a split second to reconsider my attitude about being ready to die that night and I wasn't! The only place I wanted to go was to the car and home!

We got close enough to see the cars and see the lights in the parking lot. It felt like we were safe. There's a shelter house structure in the parking area. Kenny's car and mine were the only ones there.

The shelter house has a bathroom. The whole thing is covered by a tin roof.

I said to Kenny and Gwen, "So, do you believe in bigfoot now?"

I literally had just gotten that out of my mouth when a rock came out of nowhere and hit the side of that building. It sounded like a shotgun had gone off! And then another rock hit.. and then another… and another.

We high-stepped it over to the cars, off the parking lot, but close to the cars.

I'm like, "Guys, thank you for sticking with me. Sorry I put you in this situation"

Gwen was still fooling with her phone.

Suddenly we heard up on the ridge, "Wooooop!" I looked at Gwen and said, "Please tell me you're recording this!"

She shook her head, "Yes."

I said, "Thank you God!"

Suddenly we heard, "Wooooop!" again. Then on the other ridge, "Wooooop!" We could hear them calling back and forth to each other all the way up the ridge. That strange sound could be heard echoing all the way down through there.

I was like, "This is gold!"

I'm very practical. I was thinking, *"Okay, we can get a primatologist who specializes in primate vocalizations to hear this and get it out. We have right here the proof of the existence of an unknown primate in North America! We have this! Can't deny it! Three witnesses with video."*

We looked at Gwen's phone to make sure it was still recording. It had been recording for fifty-three minutes. I said, "Okay!"

She turned YouTube Live off. What that program is supposed to do is automatically save at certain points. Autosave.

She hit, "Share." Her phone crashed, but I thought, *"No big deal. It's saved on YouTube Live,"*

I got it going again and was going to get back on YouTube Live. Suddenly her phone showed that she had only recorded for nine minutes.. The other forty-nine were gone. Disappeared. Not saved on YouTube Live as it should have been.

Gone. Gone.

There were still the three of us as witnesses. Even without the recording, we could corroborate the experience.

* * *

Three days later. I was doing an interview with a producer from a production company that works for The Travel Channel, called *These Woods are Haunted.* It used to be called, *Terror in the Woods* on Destination America. The interview was about an encounter I had eighteen years earlier.

The producer happened to ask me, "Has anything like this happened to you since then?"

I said, "Man, we had a crazy incident happen just three days ago!"

He said, "No way!"

I told him the same story I've just shared… the whole thing. He said, "I need their e-mail addresses."

I sent him Gwen and Kenny's e-mail information. I wasn't sure why he wanted them. A few days passed and we got a phone call and confirmation that we were to be flown to Philadelphia on December 14. We flew from Lexington to Philadelphia and stayed two and a half days, filmed the show for the Travel Channel's series, *These Woods are Haunted,*- Season 2, Episode 5 or 6. The tag line was, "Was it Hunting Us?

After the filming, we had to wait, and wait, and wait without expressing our anxiety to anyone. We thought the show was coming out in October 2019. Nothing was released. We had been told very strictly, "DON'T talk about this." Okay, we wouldn't talk about it. We'd wait it out.

I was in Asheville, North Carolina filming another show and I got a phone call from the producer saying, "We're airing your episode tonight. Just wanted to give you a heads up."

I had three hours to get on Facebook and try to let all my friends and family know that it was going to be on television that night. When the show came out, it was a hit and was one of the most watched episodes the show ever had. The downloads and streaming of that episode have been endless ever since.

My life, Gwen's, and Kenny's (I assume) have been wild ever since. It's been a weird ride! People I don't even know will walk up and say, "Hey, man! I think I saw you on the Travel Channel!"

Episodes of TV programs get filmed, then they must be picked up by a network who buys them and airs them. Since the episode aired on the Travel Channel, I've been crazy busy ever since. I have a packed schedule. No more Monday through Sunday 9:00 to 5:00.

If I had any advice to give anyone who wants to be on TV, I'd say, "Don't make being on television your desire. Don't go looking for it. If you have something to offer that people want, someone will find you."

I'm a hillbilly from Harlan County, Kentucky and proud to be one. I've been all over the place because of my affiliation with bigfoot research.

I've been in Washington, Northern California, and all over from swamps to the tops of mountains. I've been within feet of a grizzly bear. I've been privileged to already have seen so much!

I thank God every day that I've lived this life. If it all ended today, I'm satisfied with what I've seen. I have an amazing family and an incredible son.

I've seen things that statistically speaking, nobody gets to see, like bigfoot. The known and documented number of sightings of bigfoot around the world are about 200,000. That spans over the course of 800 years, give, or take a few. And I've seen more than one! To have had this many solid encounters in my life amazes me even without considering the statistical probability of that.

Consider that the recorded sightings number about 200,000, but the research community has concluded that only about 58% of all sightings are ever recorded. This implies that 42% of the people who have seen these creatures in the woods never tell a soul.

This type of encounter may happen to somebody late at night driving down a backroad when a bigfoot crosses in front of them. Afraid of being disbelieved or ridiculed, they never tell anybody.

Or there's the kid (me) who skipped school to go fishing on the riverbank in Harlan County, Kentucky and something rolled off the hill in front of him. This was my first sighting almost two decades ago.

Details of this encounter appear in the first *Bigfoot and Woolybooger Tales* collection of stories. What if I had never told anybody what happened? Where would I be today? Chances are that my life would have been drastically different without bigfoot.

There are days I wake up and wish it never happened. Then there are days when I wake up and thank the good Lord that it did.

I've gotten to meet so many amazing people because of my bigfoot encounters. One person was Ronald J. Morehead, who wrote *Quantum Bigfoot*. He's a hero of mine who has been researching bigfoot since the 1970s. We've become friends. I never dreamed I'd get to meet him, become friends, and have discussions with him on the phone. I've also gotten acquainted with the guys from Animal Planet's, *Finding Bigfoot*. They're great human beings. I've been blessed to meet them.

Twenty years ago, no one could convince me that bigfoot was an undiscovered species of primate. The day an individual sees a bigfoot, everything they think they knew all goes away. Thoughts about what they saw will consume them one way or another. They may be motivated to go into the woods and hope to see it again, or research the subject in depth, or they may decide after decades of hunting and being in the woods, they're not going to leave their own living room!

There's a difference between believing in something and knowing. Once a person has had a bigfoot encounter and KNOWS its real, they are consumed with that knowledge. They must either confront it, research it, or shut it down. Some people lose touch with reality after a real-life bigfoot experience.

Some might say it's a supernatural experience, or paranormal. The definition of something that's paranormal is simply that it's an event which is not of the norm.

I could drink a glass of water through a rolled-up menu and that would be paranormal to anyone who saw me do it because they drink through a straw. What I did would be considered paranormal because it's not the normal way of doing things.

Some leaders in the bigfoot community of researchers say, "Don't even disgrace the name of bigfoot by saying they are *paranormal*!" But in my context of that word, bigfoot would absolutely be paranormal because they fall outside of what is normal. So, I say that bigfoot is paranormal. It may only be flesh and blood, but it's still paranormal. This term is often used for things not understood.

The first written account of sasquatch encounters was by Viking explorer Leif Erickson. He talked about these big beasts that were swarthy, nasty, smelly creatures covered in hair. The Vikings thought they were tribe, like the Native Americans.

Apparently the Vikings encountered them living in groups and in some type of social cluster. They assumed they were a tribe of giant humans. He was interpreting his encounter with these creatures as a man contacting humanoid creatures in a new land..

The indigenous people of this continent talk about these beings in their writings. Long before the Native American stories or Leif Erikson's encounter, there are cave drawings in California that could be interpreted as bigfoot.

Christopher Columbus referred to a race of ten-foot men roaming this earth. He records the creatures he encountered on his explorations and assumes these giant-sized primates are men. He wrote about races of giants roaming the earth.

In the 1800s, Daniel Boone, explorer, diplomat, and legendary hero, and writer told a story about hunting down a "Ya-hoo." He also recorded stories from native Americans on the subject.

It is said that Daniel Boon went before the Cherokee nation to get permission first, and then came into Kentucky with the intent of finding a bigfoot. This is documented in this diary. He hunted it, found it, and killed it. He describes the creature as being extremely tall with man-like characteristics.

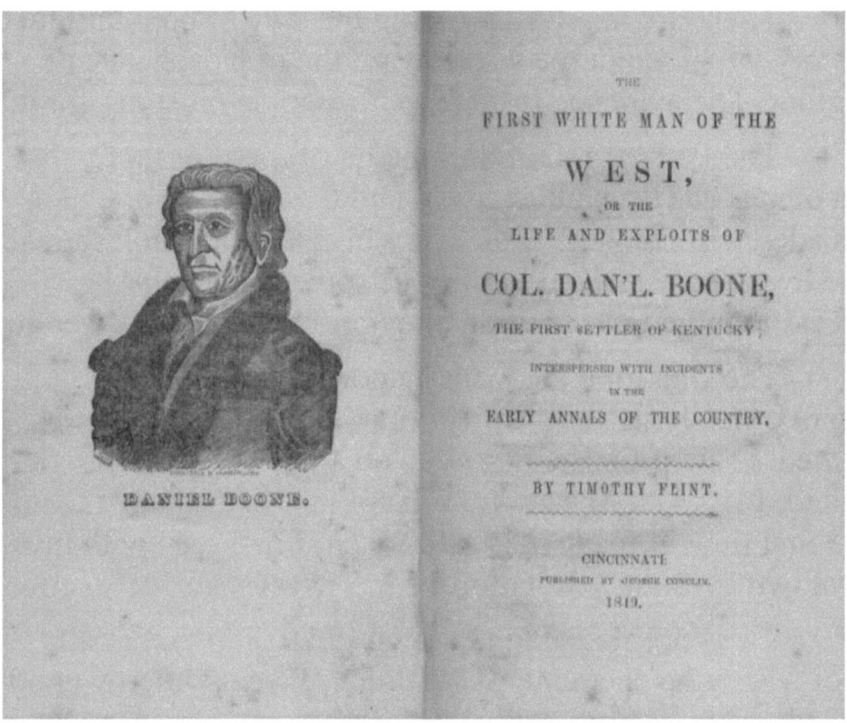

Daniel Boone and his hunting party were going to take the creature back with them to North Carolina, but it was too big. Someone said they could quarter the body of the creature. Daniel rejected that idea. He said it was too humanlike to disrespect it in that way. They examined the creature, recorded the findings in his diary, and buried it.

At one time in the early 1900s, it's been said that the Smithsonian had remains of human skeletons that were ten feet tall. This is factually recorded information. The skeletons were lost.

Some conspiracy theorists claim that the Smithsonian got rid of the bones because they didn't want to cause a public panic. It is not publicly known what happened to the skeletons of these giants. These skeletons have been referred to as the Kentucky Giants.

There are many stops along the way of pop-cultural history which point the way toward the true existence of bigfoot. The evidence is there, but a person must dig for it.

The Patterson-Gimlin footage of their bigfoot encounter has been all over TV and the internet for decades. This footage is on every bigfoot television show, and every movie about bigfoot. If someone doesn't have access to either one of these, they probably haven't seen it.

The first time I saw the famous footage was approximately in 2001, thirty-four years after it was filmed. I saw it for the first time on a television show called, *Unsolved Mysteries*. When I saw that footage for the first time, it made me realize what I had seen with my own two eyes the year before.

I was privileged to get to go in 2018 to that exact spot where the encounter was filmed. I went with my good friend and colleague, Jeffrey Ellis. Part of the reason I've agreed to do this interview is in the memory and honor of Jeffrey Ellis. He was a good friend and a great bigfoot researcher. He and I traveled the country seeing every weird bigfoot sighting place we could get to in 2018. I wouldn't have done it with anyone else.

A spur of the moment trip would literally go like this:

Phone call. "You want to go to California?"

"Sure! When?"

"In the morning."

"Let's go!"

We'd take off together on the trail of new information or a spot where a sighting had been reported. After one call we ended up four days later in California at Six Rivers National Park standing in the exact spot where Roger Patterson and Robert Gimlin stood on October 20, 1967 and recorded the legendary footage of "Patty" the female bigfoot that catapulted bigfoot into modern day culture.

If you ask most researchers, they'll tell you that unless a sighting put them into their devotion to bigfoot studies, the Patterson-Gimlin footage did. On a show called *In Search Of,* with Leonard Nemoy, the footage was first aired to the public back in the 1980s.

To have stood in the exact place where the veracity of the Patterson-Gimlin footage may eventually help prove the existence of bigfoot is truly amazing. I don't know if there will be conclusive evidence in my lifetime or in my son, Peyton's lifetime, but I believe the footage that was recorded by Patterson-Gimlin will be a crucial part of that confirmation.

Everything that's happened to me in the last twenty years of my life came about because of a bigfoot encounter of my own on a day I skipped school to go fishing at Martin's Fork located in Harlan County Kentucky.

Where's Your Bike?
S. Smith

One evening my brother and his friend were out playing and riding bikes. It had just gotten dark and he came home and fell in the door, gasping for breath.

We asked, "WHAT HAPPENED?"

"We saw something big and it followed us. And it watched us. It stood up like a man but was about seven or eight feet tall!"

We didn't know whether to believe him or not.

Dad asked, "Where is your bike?"

He said, "I ran off and left it!"

It was almost dark when they first saw this creature and it followed them but didn't get very close.

They came to a fence where they had to lift their bikes across it. Then the creature got closer and jumped the fence. That's when they ran off and left their bikes. The next morning their bikes were still where they left them.

Several days later we went to visit the neighbors and talked until it got dark. We only had a small light with us. As we started home we smelled something unusual that had a very bad odor.

We were wondering what it could be because it was a strange smell. My brother shouted, "Look!" and pointed in a direction.

There was the creature in plain sight! It was very big and stood upright like a man. It was covered in dark hair.

We stood there trying to figure out what it was. I can remember its eyes shined from the light we had. It was about forty yards away from us. We stood there frozen and it did not move. It was just looking at us.

Finally, mom said, "Let's go!" We ran home as fast as we could get there. It did not follow us.

As time went on we would be out playing and hear something walking and sticks breaking in the forest close to us. We smelled that same smell that we experienced when we saw it. We figured it was watching us. I never felt it intended to harm us, but I think it watched us a lot.

There were times our cows and horses would be bellowing and run down close to the house. They were very afraid of something.

I can also remember years later that this same creature or one like it had been seen crossing the road at the Sawmill Straight and was seen by some of the coal miners going to work at Pathfork, Kentucky.

When I was small my grandpa told me, "If you're ever out in the mountains and you smell a strong, strange bad smell, you run home fast as you can!"

I can't help wondering if he had seen it, smelled it, and knew it was somewhere out there.

Photo by Judith Victoria Hensley – Woodbooger Statue

Bigfoot
Mike Feltner (Ohio Night Stalkers)

My aunt Mickie is the person who first got me interested in bigfoot as a child. I got involved in researching and investigating bigfoot and became a full-time researcher in 1999, about twenty years ago.

On October 11, 2014 my partner Mike Miller, my son Jordan Feltner, and I were run out of an area in Adams County, Ohio by a bigfoot encounter. We have a recording of the vocals.

We turned the recording of the vocals over to David Ellis who works for the Olympic Project out in Washington State. The results were intriguing.

This documented encounter led us to be on *Terror in the Woods* on Destination America. We've also been on *Coast to Coast AM* with Connie Willis.

We go around the country speaking at bigfoot conferences. Last year we were a part of the International Bigfoot Conference in Washington State. We also have a lot of things coming up.

Because of our mutual interest in the subject, we've also become friends with Cliff Barackman from *Finding Bigfoot.*

All of that is to make the point that the public is truly interested in bigfoot. Whether they are intrigued, curious, have had their own encounter, or simply have an opinion, people want to hear about bigfoot. We've met and spoken with a lot of interesting people.

About two weeks ago we were in Washington State with Bob Gimlin, heading back to the airport. Our team went out to California for the 50th Anniversary of the Patterson-Gimlin Footage. We've become good friends with Bob. He's a great guy.

In case anyone doesn't know, he and his hunting partner saw bigfoot and the whole thing was recorded by Roger Patterson on October 20, 1967. This footage on film changed the myth of bigfoot sightings into reality.

In September we were scheduled to be at the event *Fact or Fiction* at the Horror Hound. That's in Indianapolis, Indiana. They're expecting between 35 – 40,000 people at that event. That shows how much public interest there really in this realm of possibilities.

It's a fun hobby. I enjoy the research, documentation, and the people we meet.

If anyone is interested, look for us on Facebook – The Ohio Night Stalkers. To see our episode on Destination America's *Terror in the Woods,* Episode 3, "Hunted by Bigfoots." We're on Amazon Prime, *On the Trail of Bigfoot.* We're also in the upcoming film, *Small Town Monsters.*

Face to Face
Lossie Jones

My sister-in-law, Sally Jones, and I were up on Green Branch in the woods in the fall of the year. Sally is the one who taught me all about ginseng, how to find it, where to find it, and all about it. It's not legal to dig ginseng until September. We had left the house about 9:00 a.m. that morning and had been looking for ginseng for a while. It was probably about 11:00 that morning.

About two miles past that spot is an opening in the rock. There appears to have a cave behind the opening. In front the cave, all the way down the hill, the brush had been cleaned off. It was as clean as it could be in that spot, as if somebody had cleared it and was living there.

When we went up that morning, we were hunting above the cave. As we worked our way back around, we were below the cave. There was no point in going any nearer to that spot because it had all been cleaned off and nothing was growing there.

We worked our way back toward home. We talked about how odd it was that the spot up there on the hill looked as if it had been deliberately cleaned off and it had never looked that way before. We never really thought that much about it after noticing the change in the place and wondering what was going on in that spot.

We came on down through the woods a piece. Sally found a four-prong of ginseng and it excited her to death! She screamed as loud as a don't know what because she was so thrilled to find that unusual root of ginseng. She got down on her hands and knees and was digging, trying to get the root out of the ground without damaging it.

I was standing up, behind her. Suddenly I got a whiff of a BAD odor. I didn't want to ask her if she had "tooted." I couldn't imagine any other explanation, but it was terrible! I was looking around, smelling the odor, and trying to see if there was anything or anybody else around us that might have caused the stink.

I looked up the mountain, way up. There stood a creature that looked just like a big hairy ape! It was in a clearing and my sight of it was very good. It almost looked as if it had been lit up by the light from the sky. It was looking straight at me! I was looking straight back at it.

Imagine what my heart did! It dropped! It felt like it had fallen right out of my body because it had scared me so bad!

I thought to myself, *"It's going to kill us!"*

All it did was stand there and watch us.

I couldn't get my sister-in-law to go because I couldn't make my mouth say what I was looking at. All I could manage to get out was, "Hurry! Hurry! Let's go!"

She finally got her four-prong of ginseng out of the ground, and I said, "Let's run!"

So, we started running but I still hadn't been able to tell her why. She knew something wasn't right. We slid down the hill and right into the ditch into the water, rocks, and everything. I didn't even feel it because I was so scared.

We got back to the highway and were coming down to the road, running just as fast as a human could run. It was following us down through the woods there. We could hear it breaking tree limbs as it came. It was walking and able to keep up with us running.

It followed us through the woods as we ran on the road, right down the curve above my house. That's where it stopped and went back.

Sally said, "What were you so scared of? Why were we having to run?"

I said, "BECAUSE there was a BIGFOOT standing right up there looking at us!" She never saw it.

If that creature had wanted to, I'm sure it could have covered that ground fast and gotten to us.

She said, "Don't ever tell me that kind of stuff again!"

I think the reason it came to where we were is because it heard Sally scream. She let out a blood curdling scream of excitement about the four-prong ginseng, but the bigfoot didn't know anything about ginseng. It just heard the scream and was coming to see what was going on, what was happening to us. I think it was concerned.

If a person goes out in the mountains and screams really big, that's when the bigfoot comes. It doesn't know what that scream means, so it comes to see what's going on and why someone is screaming.

That was the first time I ever saw anything like that in the woods, but not the last. Months and months later, we encountered it again. I think it may have been there watching us and keeping up with us at different times when we were out and about in the mountains. I think it got used to us and knew we were no danger and no threat to it.

If it wanted to hurt us, it could have many times because we went in the mountains a lot. I don't think bigfoot is interested in hurting anyone that's minding their own business and no threat to it or to its little ones. It's just a curious creature living among us that doesn't want to be bothered and has no desire to bother anyone else.

Another time we were up there in that same area picking blackberries off the briars that were on the side of that bank. We were up a road; what people call 24. There's an old strip-mining road up through there.

Melody, my other sister-in-law, and I were picking blackberries in July. We always went early of the morning or in the evening and stayed out of the hottest part of the day. We were picking away, trying to hurry before the sun got too hot to pick. Suddenly I smelled the same scent I had smelled months earlier when I first saw the bigfoot.

It was the same smell. Trust me when I say it is a rotten smell! It's not something anyone would want to smell and not a smell a person would soon forget! The odor will just about make a person sick by itself.

I thought to myself, *"That thing is somewhere around here, but I don't know where. I'm not going to mess with it, that's for sure."*

I told Melody about the big berries I was looking at. When I turned, the creature was standing there looking at me, no more than five feet away from us. I was looking it right in the face! I could see its features really well because I was standing right at it.

Nobody can tell me I must have seen a bear. No bear could ever stand that tall or that straight. It also had extremely long arms.

Original Artwork by Diego Martinez

It had big black eyes. Actually, they were red and black, mostly black, but I could see red in them. Its hair was fuzzy and matted. It was dirty and horrible looking, AND STINKY! It had a big flat chest with a round spot in the middle that didn't have much hair on that part, but there was hair over it like a man. It seemed to me it was muscular.

It was staring at us both, like, *"What are you doing here?"*

It was so close to me I could smell its breath. I could see its nostrils moving as it breathed in and out. It was sniffing to see what we were up to. It seemed like what I saw in his eyes was curiosity, but it still scared me to death!

I grabbed Melody by the shoulders, and I squeezed as hard as I could. I didn't want her to turn around and see what I had seen.

I screamed, "Let's get out of here!" I'm sure she could tell by the sound of my voice that I had a good reason for yelling like that.

We ran toward the Jeep. It was following us again, just like the first time I had seen the bigfoot, except this time, we could see it. As we ran, it was running through the woods parallel to us. We could see it through the trees.

That thing is so big, it must be eight or nine feet tall! I'm basing that on how close we were to it and how big it was compared to us. SHWEW! It was big! And it stinks like, I don't know what.

I've asked my friend, Thomas Marcum, about these creatures. He's an awesome bigfoot studier. He looks for all kinds of things and sometimes finds things. He looks for the creature since we told him about what happened.

He said that the creature had never tried to hurt him. It surely could have killed us out there alone with it on the mountain and in the berry patch if it had wanted to. Apparently it didn't want to harm us. To me, it acted more quizzical than anything else.

It was as if the bigfoot wanted to see what we were doing. It was just checking things out. It just stood there looking at us like, *"What are you up to?"*

It was so scary to have that huge thing staring at us and following alongside of us in the woods like that. I had the thought that maybe these big ape-like creatures are watching over us when we're in the woods. It knew we had no intention to hurt it.

Another time when we were out in the woods, we heard something we thought was that creature, although we never did see it. We suspected that's what we were listening to. It was so big and so heavy, we could hear it breaking twigs and hear the footsteps as it came through the brush, but it never did let us see it that time.

Public Domain Image

This bigfoot is a very large creature. It must weigh a lot. It walks heavy and doesn't care if it makes a lot of noise.

I've heard bigfoot holler. That sound will run chills down your spine. It's like a long wail. It's such a pitiful sound! Others in our area have heard him, also.

I really don't think bigfoot wants to hurt us. Two of the times we saw the creature, it could have if it wanted to. I think these creatures want to live peacefully and to never be captured.

I believe God put them here for a reason. I don't know what that reason is, but since they're here, I know God put them here. Bigfoots are peaceful. They just want to be left alone, make their little place to live and go about their business just like people do. I think they're curious about us, and that's all.

We always had dogs with us when we went out in the woods. The bigfoot did hurt one of our dogs. It kicked the dog. We saw the dog go flying through the air like a football. It landed down from us in the ditch. The dog had a little trouble walking after that from being kicked that far. I don't know if it tried to bite the bigfoot or what.

The bigfoot, however, never did try to hurt us.

Another time Sally and I were in that area, we were sitting down on the side of that bank having lunch. We heard something below us making little sounds. I don't know how to describe that noise. I thought of a monkey.

"What is that?" she asked. She heard it too.

"Sounds like a monkey," I said, "but you know there are no monkeys around here!"

I thought, *"Well, just go on down there and have a look."* I'm always the one who goes to see what something is. I must be the nosey one.

I stood up and walked down a little way. I ran into a very short bigfoot. It was a very short ape looking thing. I don't think it was any taller than I am.

I scared it to death, and it scared me to death! I ran and it ran. It made a weird sound as it went. I'm assuming that was a young one – a little bigfoot. It's only logical that if there was the little one, it was the baby, and there had to be a female around that had the baby.

I'm not sure if the big creatures we saw the other two times were a male or a female. An expert could probably have told by the way its ears were set, or maybe by the nose. Of course, the biggest one looked mean to me, but it might not have been. It might have been the female.

We also saw its footprints once in the wintertime. I was out of cigarettes and I had to have some. So, we had to walk out of the holler to the store. It was very cold. We had on our coats, mittens, and boggins. It was cold as ice! We didn't have a vehicle to drive. Right down by the Jim Roark Memorial Park here at Pathfork is where we saw the footprint.

The footprint was frozen in the ice. It was a bare footprint, and it was BIG. We kept thinking, *"What in the world is going on? Why is somebody barefoot in this kind of weather?"*

Nobody in the world is going to be out walking around in their bare feet in that kind of cold, and nobody has a foot that big! I could fit both of my feet inside that footprint and still have room in there. I realize I don't have a big foot (womens' size 6 ½), but that was a big track!

My sister, Julie Jones, was right there with me and she saw it, too.

One day I was in that area with my dog, Shoakie. He went running and barking up the hill toward that big rock. He was a fearless dog, but that day, when he got close to the rock, he started backing down and retracing his steps backward. Whether he smelled the scent, smelled something new, or whatever, he must not have liked it.

We didn't like the way Shoakie was acting, so we got out of there.

I'm in a wheelchair now and have COPD. I can't get back out in the mountains like I used to with my family. I would love to be able to take someone and let them get a picture of that exact spot where I first saw a bigfoot. I wish somebody already had a picture of it.

We've been by that rock so many times by the old Matt Lee place. I don't think it's a good idea for anybody to go up in there by themselves looking for the bigfoot or anything else. I don't think it would be safe.

Some people think they've turned animals out here in our area. There are bears all over the place. I don't know if they were released or not.

Bigfoot is the biggest mystery of anything I know of in these mountains. I hope nobody ever captures him. I believe he's too smart for that to happen. It's like he wants people to know he's around, but he doesn't want to ever be captured. He wants people to stay out of his space.

I think there are a lot of these bigfoot animals from one end of this country to the other. There are definitely more than one or two running around. Too many people have seen them.

A friend of mine, Darlene Kinder, told me she had seen something that she couldn't identify down where she lives at Hulen. She said one morning she came out to get in her car and startled something. She said it was huge and dark and black. She said it stood up and ran clear across the road on two feet. She said it must have been ten-foot-tall, running on two feet.

My nephew saw big tracks down by the railroad. It scared him so bad, he came home, hit the couch, and never moved off the couch all day. He finally told Sally what he'd seen. Sally and I went looking for the tracks. They had all snowed over before we got down there after he finally decided to tell it.

He was only ten or eleven, but it scared him to death to have seen naked footprints there by the railroad tracks and going up the mountain in the snow.

Some people say they think it's just a gorilla that got loose from somewhere and that's what people have seen running around here. I don't know if the same creatures from so long ago would be the ones that are still around here, but the cave is still here.

Original Artwork by Massimo Martinez

The Carving Tree
Amanda Stowers

The encounter at the Carving Tree happened in 2001. It was in Gilmer County, Georgia near the base of Springer Mountain. The place is famous as the southern terminus of the Appalachian Trail. I didn't actually see the bigfoot creature myself, but my brother who was with me at the time did.

We were on some very old family property which my dad helped manage. We were out there that day as my dad and uncle were cutting down trees for firewood. This was our main source of heat through a wood burning stove.

At the back of that family property, through the old hayfields, and near the creek was a tree they called "The Carving Tree." The name was given to it because so many people over the generations had gone back there and carved their name on this one tree. It was great. We could see carvings way up on the tree that had moved up as the tree grew taller over generations. They were so high we couldn't reach them anymore.

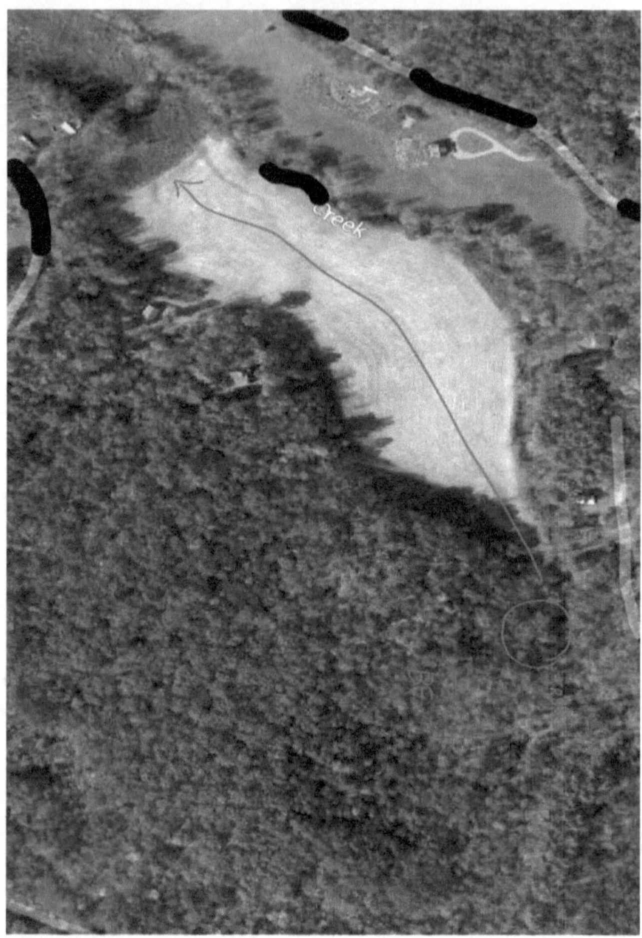

Image from Google Earth of the Hay Field Area

This is a description of the area. In a large central area were the hay fields. Probably a football field length back into the wood line was where the carving tree stood. There was a little creek that came out of the woods, down beside the hayfield.

Where the carving tree was located there was also a big overhanging rock. Underneath the rock overhang was a worn-out spot where any kind of animal could make a good nest or shelter there to sleep. It was hard packed clay.

The carving tree grew up alongside this big overhanging rock. A person had to walk around and up on the rock to carve their name on the tree.

I was fifteen at the time and my brother would have been twelve. Our uncle had recently remarried and had a stepdaughter. We wanted to take our new cousin out to the Carving Tree. We wanted to let her carve her name in the tree since she was now part of our family.

It was a sunny day. The hay was very tall.

We had made it to the Carving Tree, were showing it to our cousin, and talking. I was standing up on top of the rock and my brother and new cousin were down below the rock. My brother was looking up into the woods behind me.

Suddenly he said with genuine urgency, "We've got to go!"

I said, "No. We'll go in a minute." We'd gone all that way and I wasn't ready to leave.

He said again, "We've got to leave RIGHT NOW!"

By the sound of his voice and the look on his face, I knew something was very wrong. I jumped down off the rock.

My brother had already started running away from the tree. Our cousin was running behind him, and I ran after them. In the length of time from when we left the tree and ran to the wood line into the hay field, the creature let out a roar. It was a roar/scream/ howl. I don't even know what to call it. It was so loud that I reached up and covered my ears. I nearly fell.

The birds in the hay field all flew up and away when the creature let off that scream. The strangest part was what I learned later that day. I was the only one who heard it! Even though it was so loud to me, my brother and cousin said they heard nothing.

We continued to run across the hayfield all the way back to my uncle's house. We described what had happened to us to both my uncle and my dad. They acted like it was no big deal.

One of them said, "Yeah. Your Uncle Kerm saw a booger when he was young. They're still around."

They acted as if it was no big thing that had happened to us.

My brother described what he had seen. He said the creature was covered in brownish-red hair. It was standing in perfect posture, almost like someone standing at attention, but its arms didn't touch its side. He said the face was human, except it had hair on it like a monkey would have. He said it had no discernable neck that he could see. It was covered in hair.

There was an ominous feeling to it, like, *"Y'all don't need to be here. You need to leave!"* It was like, *"Hey! This is my area, my turf. What are you doing here?"*

My brother still stands beside this story to this very day.

He reported the encounter online to the Gulf Coast Bigfoot Research Organization (G.C.B.R.O.) This was 2001 so it was still the early days of the internet being used as a collection center for this kind of information and eyewitness encounters of bigfoot.

I would love to go back to that spot, but I've never been back to the Carving Tree since this incident. The property has since been subdivided and sold and there are houses there now that didn't exist at the time my brother saw the bigfoot. It makes it hard to go back to that spot.

From the Files of
(G.C.B.R.O.)

Reported by Confidential

RECEIVED: From the G.C.B.R.O. Web Site Submission Form

DATE: 12/16/01

TIME: About 2:00 P.M.

LOCATION: Ellijay, Georgia U.S.A.

TERRAIN: Wooded

OBSERVED: Me, my sister, and cousin were at my 2nd Cousin Eric's property. We were heading to the Carving Tree, which is a tree in the woods that the entire family has their names carved in it. Me and my sister Amanda were taking our new cousin Kelsey to the Tree to put her name on it.

When we got there, we started carving our names into the tree. After a while I started having this strange feeling that something was watching us. Since we have bears in the area I thought that we had better leave. I started to walk away. Then I turned around to tell Amanda and Kelsey to come on. As I did, I looked up the hill. I saw what appeared to be a giant fur covered man. It was only about fifty feet away. It was watching us. I turned to Amanda and Kelsey and said that we had better leave NOW.

I got out my pocketknife just for protection. When we got out of the woods and reached the field I closed up my knife and started to run as fast as I could in that field. My sister and Kelsey did the same. We ran back to Eric's truck where Eric and my dad were hauling wood.

ACTIVITIES OF WITNESS(ES): It stood about eight feet tall. It had light brown hair all over it. It looked like a human face except it had hair like on a monkey's face. It was standing in perfect posture.

DESCRIPTION OF CREATURE: There was this very weird smell, but I could barely smell it. It smelled like a roadkill skunk.

OTHER SIGHTINGS IN THIS AREA?: Not that we know of.

Note from Editor:
Amanda and her family decided to share this story publicly with identifiers for the first time as it was shared for this book, as well as the drawings. The following report to the Gulf Coast Bigfoot Research Organization (G.C.B.R.O.) is how it was originally shared anonymously.

The "Bear Skin Rug" Creature
Amanda Stowers

I had a visual experience with a very strange humanoid creature around the same time as the incidents recorded in "The Carving Tree' story on the previous pages. It also took place in Gilmer County, Georgia. I have kept the story to myself for a very long time.

I was at my parents' house, which was only about ten miles from where the Carving Tree incident happened. My three brothers, the neighbor kids, and I were all playing at a spot at the end of our driveway in the woods that we had turned into our "fort spot." We loved played outside in the dirt and in the woods.

It was a sunny day in the fall. The leaves had freshly fallen, nice and crunchy. There was a beautiful mix on the ground of light brown, orange, and red leaves. We kids were playing and having fun in the outdoors.

I was still up in the woods and the others had gone down into the driveway with their bikes

I heard a heavy rustling in the leaves behind me. As I turned, I heard something lay down, or fall down in the leaves. I looked around in a sweep to the left. As I got all the way around I noticed something weird looking back at me.

I did kind of a double take, as in, *"Am I seeing this? Is this real right now?"*

The thing I was looking at was looking back at me. It was laying down on the forest floor, arms stretched out to the side, and head laid with chin on the ground and mouth open. To me, it looked like a bear skin rug. It honestly looked like that. It's the only thing I can think of to describe what it looked like.

The creature looked very human, yet bear-like at the same time, as it had a bit of a muzzle. The creature had no ears that I could see. The eyes were black, but red at the same time, with no discernable pupils. They were like a marble. The face and body were covered in hair or fur that was the same color as all the leaves, very red-orangish-brown.

I couldn't see the creature's hands where they were positioned right behind a tree or in the leaves. The strangest thing was that from the stomach area down to where there should have been legs, there were none visible. It was like they blended in with the leaves or something.

I was frozen, still fighting in my head, *"Am I really seeing this? Is my mind making this up?"*

"No, this is real!"

I finally heard one of the other kids calling my name. I turned my head for just an instant away from the "Thing" I had been looking at. In the time it took for me to turn my head to the other kids, and then back, the thing was gone.

All this happened in less than a minute, but it felt like forever.

I'm not sure if it was a bigfoot or not.

CCO Public Domain Image - Martin Schoengaur –
Wild Man with Shield 1430

Henry County, Kentucky
Karen Byers

It's been a long time since we lived in Henry County, Kentucky. From Lockport, the location would be through town, heading west. Joe's Branch road is an old gravel road that heads out of town. The road is approximately fifteen miles long. The other end of the road comes out near Bethlehem. Our house was about seven miless down that rough road, and the house was isolated.

In the fall of 1978, we were in the house eating supper. Our house was built into the hillside. The front yard dropped off 200 feet to the raod below, then dropped again to a small creek.

Across this creek was our horse barn and chicken coope, located in a small section of bottom land. A hitching post was located to the side of this barn about three feet high.

As we were eating supper, we could hear the horses down at the barn making a lot of noise, kicking the barn and nickering.

My parents sent us down to see what was the matter. My brother and I went down the trail that led to the road. We could see down to the barn at the bottom. It was a clear moonlit night. I will never forget what we saw. A very tall, hairy creature was standing by the hitching post to the right of the barn.

The hitching post only came to its knees, and the hands were hidden by the log at the top.

My brother took off back up the hill to the house, but I stood there, maybe out of fright, and watched as it walked off. It was very tall and covered with hair. I could not make out many details, but the thing that struck me most was the long strides it took and the way it swung its arms very smooth and gracefully.

It seemed to turn its head toward me but I never at any time felt threatened. It disappeared into the trees and I could hear it as it moved uphill, but it didn't crash loudly, just the rustling of bushes. At this point I took off.

Many years before, my grandfather was clearing a hilltop about three miles up the road from the house. I can remember him saying something threw rocks at him one day, large rocks that were thrown with great force. He was a no-nonsense sort of man, but he could never explain where those rocks came from.

In 1979, my brother and I were left alone for several weeks because my grandfather was dying of cancer and my parents went to help my grandmother take care of him. We had a lot of livestock and my brother and I had to stay and take care of the animals.

My parents came home on the weekends and brought us groceries and supplies.

One night, around 8:00 or 9 p.m., we heard a sort of screaming coming from the east of our house. Our two dogs, rot terriers, hid under the bed. From the west came a similar sort of sound. My brother had a hand-held tape recorder and wanted to record the noises and let someone listen and tell us what kind of animal was making them. He was very brave and placed the recorder on the front porch, then came back in.

Whatever it was, it was the most eerie sound I have ever heard. I have heard mountain lions, bobcats, peacocks, and other wildlife, but it was not any of those. This screaming went on for 10-15 minutes, and whatever the two creatures making the sounds were, they met, and all we heard after that was silence.

We had these sounds on tape, but no one was ever able to really say what they were. One game warden said the screams came from mountain lions mating. Yet, there are not supposed to be any mountain lions in Kentucky anymore. This tape was later recorded over by my niece and unfortunately destroyed

I received a computer for Christmas one year, and my family has been fascinated by the BFRO (Bigfoot Research Organization) website. As we were sitting together and discussing some of the stories one day in February 2000, my mother and father exchanged odd looks.

When I asked them what the matter was, my father admitted they had found some huge footprints one day while they were hunting arrowheads in Hanse's bottoms.

My mother held up her hands at about 18" apart. They said the tracks were so fresh, water was just starting to seep into them. My father stated that they had never said anything to us because they did not want to scare us.

There are other stories connected to this road. There were very few people who lived close to us. Our nearest neighbors were three miles away, and at this time only two other houses on the road were lived in.

My family always believed there were more than one of these big hairy creatures in the area. There seemed to be one who was particularly smart.

We rode horses a lot at night. We often rode to the little general store in Lockport. Sometimes one of the creatures would chase us, staying just off to the side of the road in the shadows. We'd get glimpses of him and could tell he was extremely large.

Sometimes we would hear trees breaking. If we checked them out later, the broken trees would be about the size of a man's wrist and broken off three to four feet above the ground. It seemed this creature could break that size trees with little effort, like a person snapping twigs.

The bigfoot (as we came to believe it was) always stopped at the crossing before getting into Lockport. It seemed to have its own boundaries established for its own reasons. There were times it would wait for us, knowing we'd be returning home by the same road. When we got back to the spot where he stopped pursuing, he'd be waiting right there and chase/run beside us back to the horse barn. He always stopped at the hanging tree.

If this creature had wanted to harm us or our horses, it certainly could have. There were never any times that we felt truly threatened by the bigfoot, but it was very scary to know he was following or chasing in the dark. It was almost as if he was playing a game with us. He always made enough noise to make sure we knew he was there.

He'd be gone as quickly as he came without ever letting us see the direction he was taking in the night.

Original Artwork by Jordan Correll

CCO Public Domain Image

Bigfoot Sightings
Thomas Marcum
(The Crypto Crew)

Bigfoot reports make their way to me on a fairly regular basis. I'd like to share examples of an old sighting and a new one. These stories reported and documented add more bigfoot history to the area.

In the late 1950s in a place called Cary in Bell County, Kentucky two boys had a memorable experience. They were playing near a coal mine when they noticed something standing right at the mouth of the mine opening. It appeared to be a gray or white looking ape-type animal. They had never seen anything like it before and weren't sure what they were looking at. Whatever it was wasn't anything they'd seen or heard about in these mountains.

The creature was standing on two legs and had one arm hanging over a wooden cross timber. The cross timber would have been about 8-9 feet tall. The two boys ran to tell their parents, but when they got back in view of the mine opening, the creature was gone. No one had an explanation for what they'd seen.

These days were before the time when anyone would have associated their sighting with bigfoot.

In the early 2000s in Harlan County, a man I know personally was deer hunting. He was high up on the mountain and could see all around. He began using his rifle scope to scan the surrounding area for deer.

As he looked toward where an old mine opening was, he saw a large hair covered humanoid figure walking around near the mine. The creature went to the opening, ducked over, and lowered its head to walk back into the mine opening. It went inside and completely out of sight.

The person who saw this creature only told a few other individuals. He was very sure what he had seen was what most people now call bigfoot.

There have been multiple sightings in this same general area across Bell and Harlan Counties in Kentucky.

Note from the editor:

Thomas Marcum is the founder of the Crypto Crew, a cryptozoology and paranormal research organization. Thomas has over 20 years of experience investigating the unexplained.

In 2014 he was the paranormal awards winner for both picture of the year and investigator of the year.

His book *Bigfoot Witness* is full of eyewitness accounts. His latest book is *Understanding Bigfoot: Helpful Information and Answers to Common Questions*

Follow his latest discoveries at:
http://www.thecryptocrew.com

A Boy Who Saw Bigfoot
John Dixon

Recently, I've had a childhood experience with bigfoot come back to my memory. I've had a connection drawing me back to revisit that experience.

Three friends and I were at a farm where we lived in Tennessee. My sister was the caretaker of those children. The children lived on a huge farm. It borders the Cherokee National Forest and the Nolichucky River. Native Americans called it "River of Death."

There used to be a lot of Cherokee living in this area years and years ago. Their stories have been told through the years about the stuff that goes on in these mountains.

We four children were out playing, as we did many days. There was a wooded area that joined one of the fields. We went into that area to play. We were running through the woods, chasing, just playing around. We came up to a fallen log. A huge tree was down.

We went running up to the log. As we did, I saw a huge brown thing laying on the side of the log opposite us.

My first thought was, *"That's a bear! Or maybe it's a dog. It must be dead or asleep because it's not moving."*

We inched up closer to it. The closer we got to the log we finally disturbed the big hairy thing enough to wake it up. It ruffled the leaves a little as it stood up. It was large and brown in color, covered with shaggy hair. I'm guessing, but in my memory, it must have stood about seven feet tall. It was kind of hunched at its shoulders.

When it leaped to its feet, it turned and looked in our direction.

Being children, we kind of scattered, but I was frozen in place for a few seconds. It was long enough that I got a good look at the creature. Then I told myself, *"What are you doing? Get out of here!"*

I turned and ran in the opposite direction away from the creature. I made a few steps and turned as I ran, looking back over my shoulder. He was still standing there just looking at us. He didn't charge us, make any noises, or act aggressive in any way. He didn't act like he wanted to come after us at all. Clearly, he didn't want to do us any harm.

I was really frightened! I took off just as fast as I could to the edge of the wood line at the end of the field. All four of us kind of convened there together in the field, then ran on to the house.

I told my sister what had happened. "We saw a creature out there!"

We all agreed on what we'd seen. Most of the time adults will ignore children's stories about something like that.

They think they have big imaginations, especially when they are out playing in the woods. Usually, adults dismiss a child's stories as "big tales" they've made up.

Within an hour's time after that happened and we'd told my sister, every farmer in that area and a lot of men from the local town all came out to the farm.

I remember that they came heavily armed. They also came with lanterns and came with gear. The old farmhouse had a wrap-around type of wooden porch. They sat on that porch and filled it up as they came with men, lanterns, and gear. When they were all together, these men split up and went into the fields and into the woods.

The river formed a boundary between the farm and the Cherokee National Forest. This creature which I assumed to be a bigfoot had time to get back across the river and into the national forest before all those men got there and back into the mountains where it couldn't be found.

The men who had gathered were in the fields and in the woods for hours. They combed that area and searched all over. I feel certain they had to have knowledge of bigfoot being in that area. I assume a phone call was made. My sister had to have told someone to start with. The next thing we knew, there were men showing up at the farm all over the place. It was a very short amount of time between the time we told my sister and the time they started arriving. News had spread quickly.

As I remember the details, it causes me to think, *"Okay, if a child tells an adult that they've seen a bigfoot or whatever it was, the adult would dismiss it and the child would go on about their play. But once those guys showed up at the farm, so heavily armed, it makes me think they knew something already before we told what we'd seen."*

They had to know something. They had to have already heard eyewitness accounts or something that made them believe such a creature was in the area or they wouldn't have done what they did. They would not have shown up that way in full force to try to track a creature based on children's accounts of having seen a bigfoot.

They wouldn't have taken the time away from their work to come searching for a creature if they didn't already know it existed.

The only thing I know they found that night was at an old building that was used to stack hay. It was an open shed type of barn. It was way down in the field next to a huge pond. They found that bedding had been made from that hay. Evidently, bigfoot had been sleeping there.

To my knowledge, that's all they found that night. If they found it later or killed it eventually, I never knew anything about it. I hope they didn't, but it would have been nice to know what happened to the creature after that day.

I have no one to ask at this point. All the men who were there, have no doubt died out. I'm 54 now and was a child when this event happened. There's really nobody I know of to ask. If I did find someone, I'm not sure they'd even be willing to talk about it.

I'm convinced those farmers knew something or they wouldn't have come running to help search the way they did. There's no way a bunch of farmers, as busy as farmers are, would have just dropped everything and come rushing out there with guns and lanterns based only on a children's account of what we had seen.

They set up stations and checked that place out for hours.

Somewhere, there's probably family members still alive of these farmers from that area who have heard the tales, or heard about that night's events, but I have no idea of how to find them.

Living near the national forest, I've heard all kinds of stories about different things. But this is my own personal experience.

We didn't go back in the woods for some time after that day. I don't recall being told not to go back in the woods but since that encounter I have been very cautious. Even now I sometimes get the sense that I don't belong in certain places. I can sense things.

I have always been gifted to sense things around me so, as a kid through adolescence, emerging adulthood and now I just don't put myself in the position to find out what those inner warnings may be protecting me from.

I believe there are bigfoot creatures out there. I believe they are biological creatures. These forests are so vast and these mountains so big, I believe there are many living creatures that man has yet to put his hand on. I think God has created things in this world, and in these woods, that they've just not found yet because the animals are smart enough to survive over time. They use defense mechanisms to stay hidden from human's prying eyes.

People can laugh or whatever they want to do, but when a person has an experience, it's THEIR experience and they know what happened. They KNOW what they saw.

Photo of the Woodbooger Statue at High Knob in Norton, Virginia by Judith Victoria Hensley

Northern Kentucky Bigfoot Activity
Thomas Shay
(Northern Kentucky Bigfoot Research Group)

Around June 3, 1962 there was a rash of bigfoot sightings here in Trimble County, Kentucky. They called the creature "The Trimble County Thing."

It looked in windows. It killed livestock.

There was a big hunt to find this creature. The state police, the sheriff's department, tracking dogs, and local farmers all got involved. A couple of the local radio stations had helicopters at that time. The hunt was on hot and heavy for about a month, then it died down.

Over the years the interest in the creature picked back up. I was not one of those people. Honestly, I didn't believe in bigfoot. The first time I saw one, it completely threw me off balance. I hadn't really thought about evolution and the number of species on the earth. It freaked me out a little bit.

I had my own encounter to solidify things.

I was home on leave from the army and was on my way to see my girlfriend. This big unidentified creature crossed the road right in front of me down by the Ohio River. I turned the car around and came back to check it out. I got out of the car and followed it! I wanted to make sure I was seeing what I thought I was seeing.

It was reddish brown, and about 7 ½ feet tall, or something like that. I'm only estimating on the height of this one. I had nothing to measure it by except my own height.

It realized I was following. It turned around and kind of growled and yelled in my direction. That was enough for me. I turned around and got out of there and went back home.

My parents said, "Thought you were going to see your girlfriend."

I said, "Let me tell you what I saw." So, I told them what had happened and said, "I'm not going anywhere. Not tonight."

I've been doing research since 1987 after I had my first encounter..

I have seen at least two of these creatures. They are flat faced and don't look like an ape. Honestly, their appearance is more man-like. They have a flat nose and hair on their face, but not like some of the descriptions of bigfoot others have made.

In February 2015 I found some prints. I was making plaster casts of them. While I was concentrating on this, bent down making the cast, I had one walk up on me – within about 30 feet. When I realized he was there, I didn't move; I didn't do anything.

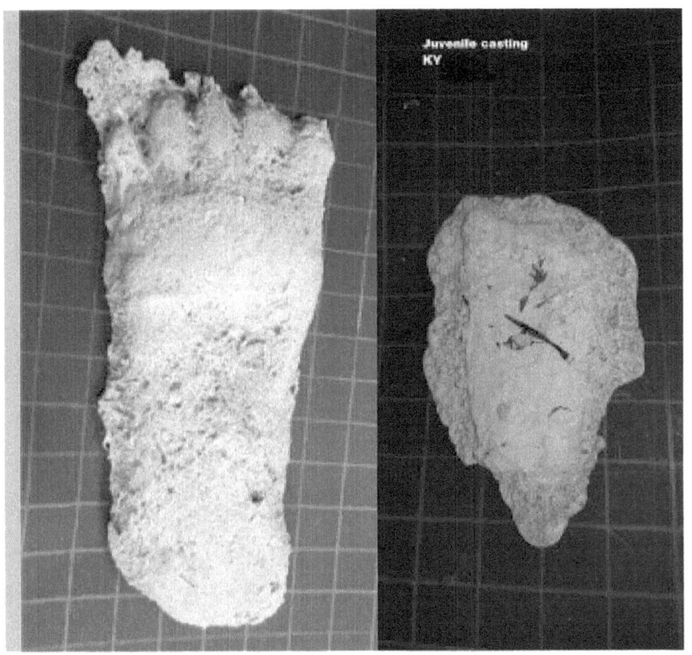

My four-wheeler was in between me and the creature. I had left my handgun on the four-wheeler because it got in the way while I was casting. I thought about making a dash for the four-wheeler, then I changed my mind and stayed right there.

It looked at me for what felt like an eternity, but it really wasn't. It was looking at me and I was looking at it. Slowly, it turned around and sniffed the air, then walked down the ridge. He was reddish brown.

When I took people back with me to the location to investigate, we measured from a tree limb that the top of his head hit to get an approximate height where I'd seen him standing. He was about 8 or 9 feet tall. We call him Goliath. The footprints are about 21 inches long.

Usually they seem to be curious creatures, but we've had some incidents where things got a little hairy. We've had things thrown at us very violently. On one occasion we didn't realize there were two or three of them around our basecamp. They were screaming. One of them slapped the side of the trailer and left a handprint – a big greasy handprint. I have pictures of it.

A lot of researchers come in and walk through the woods like they're chasing something. For the research we do, we go in and set up a base camp. We wait for them to come to us.

They do come up to our basecamp. We had one walk within 15 feet of our basecamp one night. We also got a night vision video of another one crawling up to us, checking us out.

Two weeks ago, we were out on the trail and we walked up on one. The property owner was with me and one of my team members. When the property owner saw the bigfoot, he ran back to basecamp.

There are ten of us who do bigfoot research together in this area. They are all good people.

We do limited searches in the daytime. We do NOT go out or send people out in the middle of the night. We usually search within a hundred yards of our basecamp. Nobody goes out at night because it's just too dangerous. We don't go in national parks or state parks. We do our searches on private property where people have seen these things.

I believe these hominids live in family groups. We've seen big ones and young ones. We also saw a female that was distinguishable because it had breasts.

The following information is used from the website of Thomas Shay – Northern Kentucky Bigfoot Research Group.

Originally published June 16, 1962
Trimble County Sheriff To Lead Search For Beast POLICE DOGS, HELICOPTER, POSSE TO BE USED IN ANIMAL HUNT TODAY
<u>Courier Staff Report</u>

Friday, September 12, 2014 11:00 AM

WALKIE-TALKIES FOR BEAST HUNT — Sheriff Curtis Clem checks portable radio equipment with state trooper John Miller (in police car) in preparation for today's all-out hunt for "the thing" that has residents of northwest Trimble County scared. The sheriff has asked all persons desiring to join the hunt to register with him since vicious dogs will be used that could seriously injure anyone not in the party. Radio units are being provided by the Madison Radio Service here.

There is some form of animal still loose in the northwest part of Trimble County - be it a gorilla, bear, lion or large dog - no one seems to know for sure, but many are sure something is there that doesn't belong, and they want it eliminated.

With this thought uppermost in mind, Sheriff Curtis Clem is leading an extensive search later Saturday for "the thing," as Trimble County people seem to refer to it.

"We'd like to get it alive if possible, or dead if necessary. But we want to be sure he's removed or run out of this area," the sheriff said today. "These people are scared, and they want action," he added.

So a large number of men, equipped with keen eyes and rifles powerful enough to drop almost any kind of beast that could prowl this area, will set out sometime later today to see if the trail of the beast can be found, and if it can be capture or killed.

A helicopter overhead will aid greatly in following the animal at high speed should it be flushed from the dense undergrowth.

A gang of seven highly-trained vicious police dogs will accompany the hunt. They will be brought by a special dog trainer from Louisville, who offered the services of his dogs when he first saw the reports of the beast in his newspaper.

Many people seem skeptical and wonder why it isn't seen more than it is. But others point out that the ground being roamed by the beast is wild territory, and that it could be hiding in deep caves protected by large rocks or could be nestled in the dense thickets.

Sighting reports continue to be turned in to Sheriff Clem. The latest story comes from Mrs. Derrell Corley, who lives on the Kidwell Pike. She said that sightings of a beast were not a new thing to members of her family. She said that about three years ago some type of an animal would lurk in the weeds and high grass and thump along after her children when they went for the cows. "It made all sort of weird noises," she said.

About this time the Corley family was raising a garden containing melons. "We'd never get a whole melon before that animal or whatever it was, would get to it. It looked like a human hand had scraped the heart out of each melon," she said.

"One time my daughter Mary went to the garden and looking up, saw a black thing that looked like a small monkey or chimpanzee standing in a corn row. As some other children were coming, she looked first to the kids, then back to the spot, and the beast had disappeared," she said. Later that year similar reports came from Patton's Creek, only a few miles from the Corley place.

Most common among the sighting reports of the beast are stories that it looks like a chimpanzee or a gorilla. Some prints in the mud that had been found were taken to a Hanover professor and were termed those of a large dog. But the prints were found near a spot where the beast is believed to have been. The prints could easily be those of a dog, and still not the prints made by the beast.

Up to the present time there were still no further reports of either personal injuries or animals being killed since the early report of the death of a calf. But the sighting reports continue, and as do reports that dogs return to farms with every indication of having been in a vicious fight.

Sheriff Clem hopes the best hunt today brings the good news that the beast is no more, and that Trimble County residents can go back to living a normal, safe life.

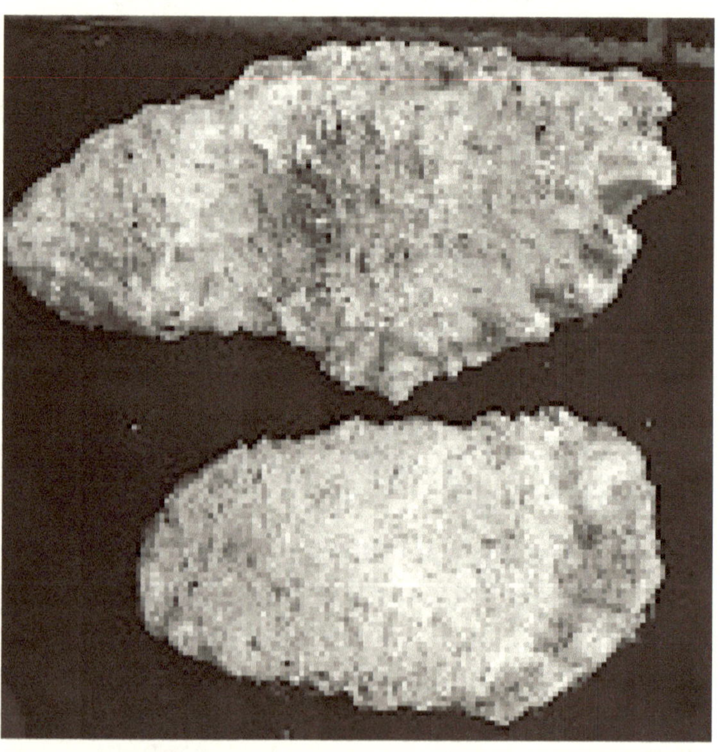

Photos Used with permission from the website of Thomas Shay

June 18,1962

Originally published June 18, 1962

'The Thing' Eludes Hunt In Trimble

FARMERS REPORT 3 SHEEP KILLED; DOG SLASHED; NO TRACE IS FOUND

Courier Staff Report

Friday, September 12, 2014 11:00 AM

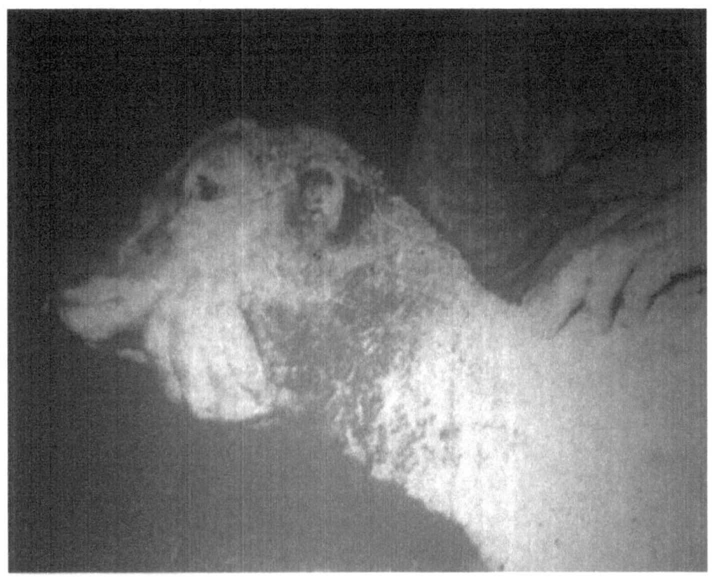

SEEING IS BELIEVING: Lawrence McDowell, son of Trimble County Farmer Lester McDowell, holds his father's sheep that was attacked and cut on the head by an unidentified animal believed to have been "the beast." Three other sheep owned by McDowell were previously found dead from attacks.

"The Thing" is still at large in Trimble County, Kentucky, but it is believed to have been flushed out of the Kidwell Pike area northwest of Bedford and moved into a section five to six miles southwest of Milton.

According to a report today from Trimble County, the alleged beast has at last resorted to killing livestock.

Trimble County Sheriff Curtis Clem said he didn't know what the next step would be, following a five and a half-hour unsuccessful search for the mysterious animal Saturday night.

The sheriff's party combed the Kidwell Pike area Saturday from about 7:00 p.m. until after 12:30 o'clock yesterday morning.

It is believed their quarry was flushed out of this section of the county as the result of activities of hunters and a sharp increase in automobile traffic at night with accompanying headlight glare.

During the weekend, the sheriff was told that a beagle hound owned by Earl Grant, who resides at the foot of Craig Creek Hill, was found dead with its throat ripped and other cuts on its body.

Lester McDowell, a resident of the same neighborhood, reported three of his lambs had been killed since Wednesday. His son Lawrence told a Courier reporter that two of the lambs had ripped throats, heads were crushed, and all blood had been drained from their bodies. A fourth had been found injured but was still alive.

One of the animals was found Thursday, another Friday, the third Saturday and the fourth yesterday.

An attack by dogs was discounted due to the manner in which the lambs had been killed.

The lamb's incidents occurred at a point about five miles east of where "The Thing" had allegedly been seen last week, which led to belief that it had moved out of its former place of concealment.

McDowell had not reported his first losses earlier because he has no telephone and had no occasion to make a trip to town until Saturday.

A number of farmers contact by The Courier representative were asked opinions as to why the strange animal had for the first time resorted to killing live stock, although it may have been in their area for the past two or three years.

All though the viciousness results from Owen Powell having sicked his dogs on it and it may have been wounded, also that hunting activity and auto headlights may have been a contributing cause.

There is no general agreement that a dangerous animal of some kind is at large in the county.

Results from hair samples
Thomas Shay
Northern Kentucky Bigfoot Research Group

On September 7th, 2018 Cliff Barackman and James Bobo Fay visited my home to document my casting collection. I told them that I had some hair samples and Cliff said if I wanted he could let Dr. Jeff Meldrum analyze them.

I gave the four samples to Cliff. On September 22, 2018 Cliff contacted me by phone and said that two of my samples matched a gold standard set by Dr Henner Fahrenbach the leading authority in Sasquatch hair.

The hair was collected in my research area in Trimble county KY.

Below is the email I received from Dr. Meldrum.

Sometimes our hard work in Bigfoot research pays off.

Jeff Meldrum

to me

Tom:
Cliff has been sharing with me some of his dialogue with you. he is quite impressed with the data you have been collecting. We mounted some of the hair samples and

were quite excited about one of those in particular. It had all the hall marks of the Gold Standard set by Henner Fahrenbach some time ago.

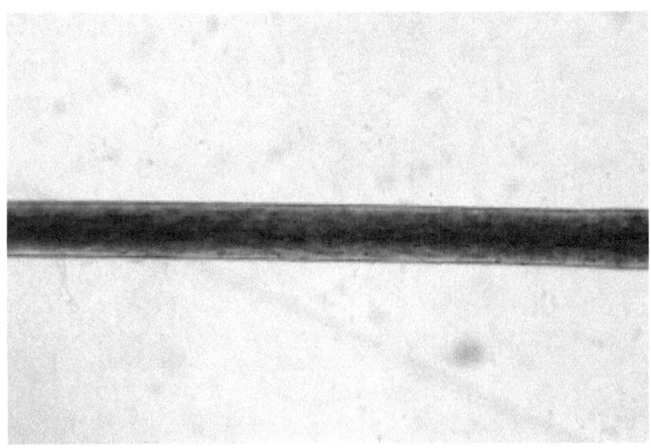

There is your sample above, and another suspected sample from elsewhere

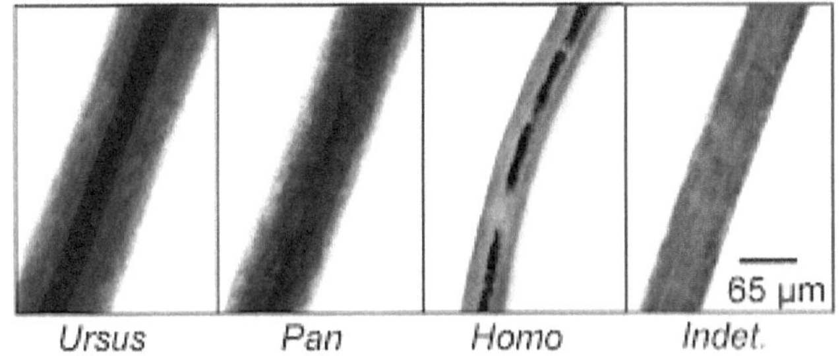

I look forward to hearing more from you.

Jeff
Jeff Meldrum, PhD
Professor of Anatomy & Anthropology
Dept. of Biological Sciences
Idaho State University

The following stories are Printed with permission from
Thomas Shay
Northern Kentucky Bigfoot Research Group

Martinsville, Indiana 01-16-2014

I just finished taking a report from a gentleman who wishes to stay anonymous (name and address on file). Report as follows:

This sighting took place on January 16, 2014 after a day of squirrel hunting along the west bank of the White River across from the power plant.

"It was getting late in the afternoon and I was exiting the woods when I noticed this large shaggy hairy thing that was squatting near the riverbank.

At first I thought it was a bear. As I stood there and watched this thing, it suddenly stood up and looked right at me for a few seconds which seemed like an eternity.

It made a "humph" sound, turned and disappeared down the riverbank."

Tom: Can you describe what you saw in detail?

Witness: Yes, I can. It had dirty brownish red hair which looked as it was matted and littered with debris. It stood between 7-8-foot tall and had a build of a professional body builder except its arms was longer than ours. It also appeared to have a slouch as it stood up.

Tom: When it moved off did it run?

Witness: No! It moved off down river as if it weren't worried about me.

Tom: What do you believe you encountered?

Witness: I don't know what I saw. I'm still having a hard time understanding it.

Tom: Do you think it may have been a Bigfoot?

Witness: Before this happen if someone would tell me the same story I would laugh and tell them they were nuts. Yes, I believe it was a Bigfoot!

Tom: Have you gone back to the area to check for prints ?

Witness: NO!

Tom: Why?

Witness: If this was a Bigfoot then its way bigger than me. and I have no idea what I'm dealing with.

The witness requested we stop the interview. The witness talked with me off the recorded a little more about his encounter. The witness agreed to take me to the site.

I know the area where this encounter took place. In the late 1990s I conducted two investigation's in Monrovia, Indiana.

I believe the witness did encounter something on the riverbank he cannot explain. Morgan Monroe Forest is close by with several sightings and encounters in the area. An investigation should be conducted in the area as soon as the weather breaks.

The Marble Hill Monster – Friday, January 10, 2014

In southern Indiana in the southwestern part of Jefferson County on the outskirts of the small town of Handover is a place called Marble Hill. It is the site of the failed nuclear power plant back in the 1970s. The area was plagued with a rash of sightings and encounters. Some frightened people were run out of the woods. Homeowners were harassed in their homes. Parked couples in cars were attacked by a large hairy bipedal monster as descried by the witnesses at the time. This lasted off and on for about four years and then the sightings and encounters stopped, and the Marble Hill Monster was soon forgotten.

In the spring of 2012, a young man was mushroom hunting in the Marble Hill area when he caught sight of a large bulky hairy creature standing in the wooded area he was in. The witness was not more than seventy-five yards away, at which time it screamed at him.

At this time, the young man was so frightened he began to run from the creature. While running he noticed that it was chasing him. After exiting the wooded area, he reached his vehicle and made his escape. He peered in the rear-view mirror and saw what appeared to be an eight-foot hairy man like creature.

In June 2013 two fishermen were bass fishing in the Ohio River below Marble Hill. They observed a seven to eight-foot hairy bipedal creature on the riverbank.

In September 2013, a witness had a sighting on Marble Hill Road.

In October 2013, a hunter sighted large hairy creature.

In December 2013 vocalizations were heard in the Marble Hill area.

These reports came firsthand from the witnesses who met with us at the show. Marble Hill is just across the river from Trimble County Kentucky. An investigation is warranted in the Marble Hill area.

Morton Ridge road incident 09/17/2019

On September 18, 2019, I received an email concerning what looked like a bigfoot on Morton Ridge Road in Trimble County, Kentucky where the witness almost hit it with his vehicle. This took place on the evening of September 17, 2019. I contacted the witness and we agreed to meet on the 23rd at the sighting location.

At 11:30 a.m. I met with the witness near the location. After a brief introduction, we proceeded to the location of the incident. The location isn't exactly on Morton Ridge but at the end where Wises Landing Road begins. Immediately the witness began to tell me what occurred the evening of 09/17/2019.

Witness:

It was a little after 9:00 p.m. I was traveling west on Morton Ridge Road. As I came to the end where it starts going downhill onto Wises Landing Road, this thing steps out onto the road. At first I thought it was a person. As the headlights came fully upon this thing, it stopped in the center of the road. That's when I came to a full stop. It appeared to be struggling to look my direction through the headlights. As I watched, it then continued across the road and on down the hill. After getting home I remembered reading about some stories here in the county and started looking online and found your Blog then emailed you.

During the interview we recreated the events while he was in his vehicle and did a height comparison of the creature he saw. I measured it to stand around 7 feet tall and around 3 1/2 feet wide at the shoulders The witness described the creature as reddish in color and that it stood and walked upright as a man.

The witness also stated that he has driven this route for several years at night and has never seen anything like it before. Upon investigating the area, I found no visible signs of fresh tracks. The substrate was hard and dry due to the drought conditions.

Also, the path of the creature described by the witness moved from north to south along a power line brake. The area is hilly and forested.

Upon further investigation of the area my wife and I found an old trackway that appeared to be traveled extensively. The prints measured 16 1/2 inches long. I will conduct several investigations in the area and hope to do some weekend expeditions on site.

The area has a long history of sightings. The witness is sincere in what he reported. The witness did not want to be videotaped or have his name made public but stated that he would be available for more questions.

My Daylight Sighting 8/11/2017

On 08/11/2017 at 4:30 p.m., I was traveling south on US 421 with my family. At 2.4 miles out of Bedford, Kentucky ahead of us a figure crossed US 421 from east to west. It went over the guard rail and down the bank with such speed and agility!

When I reached the site of the crossing and looked down into Town Branch Creek it was still standing in the creek bed. It stood over 6 feet tall. The hair was long, matted and unattended - what one would call messy bed head hair. The color appeared patchy dark reddish brown with some bright red orange.

As I was paying more attention to it instead of the road I almost ran off the road. After gaining control of my vehicle I found a place to turn around and proceeded back to the spot, at which time the figure we saw was gone.

Note:

We have investigated and documented several reports of sightings and encounters in this area. Charlie Raymond of the Kentucky Bigfoot Research Organization documented an encounter in the same area a few years ago.

I'm returning on 08/12/2017 for a follow up on any evidence found.

Sighting 10/14/18
Today's date: 10/15/18
Date of encounter or sighting: 10/14/18

The incident took place around 2:00 p.m. on a cold, lightly raining day.

We have access to a research area for this group. We went in through their main trail with my cousin to go check some cameras. We made it about 20 feet from the road and he said that he saw something down in the gully.

It seemed to be somewhere from 5-8 feet tall. I told him that it was just their decoy, but when we got to the top of the hill the decoy was in the same spot. So, we continued to the cameras.

When we got there, I had him pull the ards and I got up in the stand to make sure the straps weren't rotted away. I got up there and looked around and saw something tall standing on two legs. It seemed to be at least 7 feet tall and about 100 yards away from us.

I had my cousin come up there with me and we watched it turn away and leave. After that we left in a hurry. I believe that we caught his attention, and it was curious to know what we were doing. So, it followed us.

Note:

This happened in my research area. On the last expedition one of the members also saw a dark figure moving through the woods. On one of the trail cams there was a photo of a figure.

Also, with another researcher on a couple of trips in, he captured some nice vocals and tree knocks. I have also casted several prints. The hair that Dr. Meldrum stated to have all the hallmarks of the Gold Standard set by Henner Fahrenbach came out of this location.

I will be conducting an expedition November 2nd 3rd and 4th 2018 in this location.

December 6, 7, 8 2019 Expedition - Trimble County, Kentucky

Wow! Our expedition of December 6th, 7th, and 8th yielded some interesting results.

On the first night, after placing our four cameras and DVR system, we captured some interesting footage which will be shown after I completely review all the video recordings.

Around 6:30 pm on Friday night, Shelia placed her audio recorder, around 100 feet behind base camp, where she heard a loud clap. Later after she reviewed the audio recording and heard the loud clap also a few whoops, distant howls, and knocks.

We were able to capture these on other audio devices Friday night into the early hours of Saturday morning.

At around 8:30 am Saturday morning, the landowner walked back to our basecamp. He informed us that back on the trail he found what appeared to be a footprint crossing the trail. We immediately investigated the print.

The print was 12 inches in length with some toe detail. Upon further investigation we found several other prints moving into the woods by the same individual. Jan Ehl documented said print with photos and then casted said print.

Saturday night not much happened - a few knocks and a distant vocal. Things didn't get exciting until around 2:30 a.m. Sunday morning. At the time most of us were half asleep and wrapped up snug, keeping warm close to the fire.

We heard something large circling basecamp and suddenly something huge, moved down the hill, stomped thru the leaves. It broke large limbs laying on the ground as it stomped off. This was at least 10 to 15 feet behind Keith Loftin and me.

It kept itself just outside the light of the fire. By this time everyone in basecamp heard it and were scrambling for their thermals and night vison cameras. It moved off quickly into the night. We thermed the area to no avail. Ben Taylor did use his thermal on the ground where we observed the heat signature of its foot falls, which appeared bipedal.

The rest of the morning was uneventful after that. Keith Loftin and I will continue to review the rest of the audio and video.

Note: We did capture something close to the audio equipment. It can clearly be heard - something exhaled next to the parabolic dish which was 100 feet outside basecamp. There was also a loud growl and grunt.

We are planning another expedition. We will try and get the evidence posted soon.

Strange incidents in Carroll County Kentucky, 2005 through 2020

Some strange incidents have been occurring on a farm in Carroll County Kentucky from 2005 to 2020. There have been several people who talked about seeing something in this general area. Yesterday I went to the area and was able to talk with one of the individuals who says reports seeing something and get somewhat of a look at the area before being called away.

The individual's description of what has been happening follows in their own words:

"We have a farm in Carroll County and have lived there since December 2005. The first winter we had some 'happenings' but none were substantiated. I wrote to T. Shay and he posted the story.

I found what appeared to be a questionable track in the spring of 2006. Other than that, there has been no real activity until recently.

A few weeks ago, we noticed increased coyote activity – howls and yips mostly. We went to Glauber's to get some traps. One of the ladies there told us that they had sold well over 100 traps in just a few weeks. She said this was a record for them.

When we first moved to the farm, we would sometimes get the feeling that we were being watched. That went away when the odd activity stopped. Now, in the past couple of weeks, we have noticed several times that the farm had a certain 'feel' to it.

We noticed little things. I heard what sounded like a tapping on a window one night. Later I heard what sounded like a larger animal moving around. In the morning, our miniature horse was in front of the house, so I assumed it was him.

I blew off the tapping as a bird or cat – something along those lines.

We have also been having the feeling that someone was up by the house when we weren't around. Our house is difficult to get to and secluded. There's no reason anyone would be up there. Because of this, we began to check tracks on our driveway and other paths people would use to get to our house.

This past weekend (2/29-31) I noticed what appeared to be a barefoot track about the size of my foot. I wear a size 9 shoe. I looked at it closely. It appeared slightly deeper than my tracks were. I weigh 130-135 pounds. I looked around and saw another track which appeared to be another left foot. This one had the impression of 5 toes. The first only seemed to have 4 with a hint of the 5th.

The stride length was close to mine when I am walking. I am 5'6". I marked the tracks as I had other things I had to do, and had the intention of coming back to take pictures, measure and take a good long look to see if it was possibly just an overlap of boot prints with my dog's prints. It rained a short while later and the tracks were washed out.

Monday, 3/2

A friend of ours needed me to bring something down the hill to our 'parking lot'. I was walking the driveway which is about ½ mile long with trees on both sides. Heading down the hill, there is a valley to the right and the hill goes up towards the house to the left.

I had my .22 rifle due to the coyotes. I began to hear a 'squeaking' sound to my right. It sounded about halfway down the valley. It almost sounded like a mouse squeak but coming from a larger animal. I had never heard it before.

I admit that I was a little frightened. I called out something like, "Stay away! I'll shoot!"

Right after I said that a large limb came from somewhere and hit some downed trees and branches. It hit with force. It was windy that night, so that could have been it. But something has bothered me about that and as I was typing, it hit me what it was. I don't think the way the limb fell, and the direction of the wind matched.

I hesitate to say for sure, since I am fully aware my mind could be playing tricks, but it seems to me that is what has bothered me about the limb.

The squeaking never stopped except for a second maybe after the limb hit the deadfall.

I decided that my .22 wasn't going to be much help, so I rushed on down the hill.

Late Tuesday night, early Wednesday morning, some friends were coming up the hill in their truck. The truck wouldn't go into 4X4, so they stopped to see if they could fix it. She was holding the light so he could see.

She heard something large that appeared to be coming toward them. It stopped several yards away. She kept looking back and saw yellow eyeshine a couple of times. I asked her how high off the ground and she indicated between 3-4 feet.

I asked her how far apart and she indicated 6-8 inches. I didn't get any more details. I will update if I get more.

They got their truck fixed and came on up. I had not told them about any of the other stuff that had happened until she told me about this.

Last night was Thursday 3/5. Nothing much happened. I thought I heard a couple low growls, and we did feel like something was watching us. The growls were on the edge of my hearing though and most likely are something else.

There was a scratch on the same window that I had heard the tapping. There were a couple of odd sounds outside like something walking into stuff. But nothing more definitive. Admittedly, I was a little jumpy. This time I decided to go ahead and get this info to T. Shay.

I don't pretend that any of this is proof. I have little but my word to speak as 'evidence'. I make no claims as to what this could be, and I readily admit there are rational explanations for all of it.

On the other hand, some of the things that have happened are like reports of suspected activity.

Note from the editor:

Thomas Shay is the founder of the Northern Kentucky Bigfoot Research Group. His first personal encounter with the elusive creature in 1987, impacted Thomas's future and his search for evidence and truth about bigfoot.

It has been reported that Mr. Shay currently possesses the largest collection of original Bigfoot cast east of the Mississippi.

He is endorsed by Cliff Barackman of the Discovery Channel's popular show Finding Bigfoot as being one of the best researchers in the country. Thomas appeared on Finding Bigfoot season 5, episode 1

Thomas is well established and respected in the bigfoot world and continues his bigfoot research and field investigations. Thomas lives in Trimble county Kentucky, with his wife and son.

*Photo of the Woodbooger Statue at High Knob in Norton, Virginia
by Judith Victoria Hensley*

Bigfoot Yell
Sherry Roark Daniels

My husband Jay Dee, my little dog Milo, and I had driven up the road to an old strip mining site. It was the same area where we had seen a black panther.

We stopped to let Milo out to go potty. Jay Dee decided to do a bigfoot yell. I don't think we expected anything in response

Something hollered back at him! It was like, "Woooaaaahhh!"

We all heard it clearly. Even our dog Milo came to alert when we heard it. We didn't go looking for whatever it was.

Hearing it was enough.

Original Artwork by McKenna Hollywood

Bigfoot in Indiana

Matthew McGuire (Bigfooting Indiana)

The first time I ever had any knowledge of bigfoot was around 1978 or 79. I was about 8 or 9 years old at the time.

We were in Brown County Indiana and we had been spending some time with family there for a couple of weeks. My cousin, some friends of his, and I decided we'd go out in the woods and play close to where my aunt lived.

We went out there and were walking along following this small trail out through the woods. The little boy in front of me stopped. I stepped around him to go on past, overlooking down into a valley.

When I passed him, a bigfoot jumped down from my left. I don't know if it had been hanging on a tree, sitting on a ledge, or what. I did not see it when we were walking on the trail. It landed on two feet straight in front of me and stood straight up.

I felt the wind off it when it jumped and went past me.

I was looking at its leg or something and saw long dark hair. As best as I can remember, the length of the hair was about 4 inches long and super coal black.

When it stood back up, it immediately went off to my right into the underbrush there.

That childhood incident is what got me started in this bigfoot research. I've told people as an adult, "I literally had bigfoot jump into my life!"

I'm 52 years old and for the better part of 40 years I've had encounters and sightings all over the state of Indiana. A good friend of mine, Jay DeFord, is the one who got me started going back out in the woods again.

I had one encounter in Fort Stewart Georgia when I was in service. We were in night maneuvers and there was a bigfoot that walked up beside of the road. We couldn't see it, but we could hear it. I knew what it was. It stopped on the other side of the road across from us. It stayed there a little while, then took off.

After that, I really didn't have anything else go on until after I got out of the service and got back to Indiana. I got with a buddy of mine who lives in the Indianapolis area. He had a place he liked to go camping all the time. We started going down there.

That was several years ago. I would have to say that if we ever got close to where a family/group/clan of them were together wherever they were holding up at, we had to be really, close.

We started camping in this same place of about 70 acres in Brown County. We had everything happen there.

We had a couple of juveniles come into camp one night while we were laying there in our tent. We could hear them out there playing with the coolers and other stuff.

It was the first time I ever heard the juveniles at play. I've heard people say that the young ones will "cut up and play."

Their laughter sounds like a kid's laughter. That was the first time I ever heard it. I can tell you that it's for real. They sounded like little kids out there laughing and playing around.

We didn't hear anything else out of them but playing around in our stuff and the laughter. I didn't want to open the tent for fear of spooking them and them running off. I just wanted to listen to them. Also, we didn't know if there was an adult out there with them watching over them.

I thought it was best not to disturb the situation, but to continue to listen. The whole thing really caught me off guard. The way we knew for sure that what we were hearing truly were juvenile bigfoot was that after about half an hour or 45 minutes of this, it ended.

The next morning at daybreak we got up and proceeded to hike on back into the property. That's when/where we found tracks. The tracks were very small. I'd say the smallest set was around six inches long and probably close to 3-4 inches in width. They were wide. They looked like a squared off footprint.

They weren't like a human footprint where you can see the instep. They were more like the adult bigfoot tracks we've found over the years, but a lot smaller.

The next set of tracks we found close to the little ones were in the eight-inch range. They were all over the hillside back in that property. In that location is where my buddy found an adult track that measured more around fourteen inches in length.

I said, "Stay right here by this track. I want to see if I can find the next step. We need to figure out how far the next step is."

I kept looking around intently until I finally found it. The stride between the first step and the next step was around 5-6 feet apart. I don't know if it was running back through there or what. It was quite obvious that the first print was from a right foot. The next print that I found was straight out from it of the left foot. There were broken saplings all over the place.

My buddy was like, "They've had windstorms down here and stuff."

I said, "No. The wind is not going to hit right here in this one spot. You know? Look how fresh all of this is! It had to have happened last night or early this morning."

In that same place we heard a howl one night in the back valley. That was impressive. It was so guttural! It had to take a lot of lung power to make that level of a howl. We listened to that for about 10-15 minutes. We had everything there – finding tracks, broken saplings, and howls. We also had a tree limb thrown at us one night at the camp site.

It was probably about five years ago that my wife, Dawn, and I decided to go back to that same place. I wanted to show her the property where we'd been camping at and having all the experiences.

It was late spring or very early summer when I took her down there. Foliage was still down. The grass was still golden and brown, not having come back to life yet that spring. We went and walked the trail.

I told her, "Be very quiet. I'm just curious."

I don't even know why I thought about us being quiet as we walked the trail.

"We need to be quiet and not be making much noise, stepping on leaves, twigs, and stuff. I want to show you the first valley."

There were two valleys on the property As we got back there, we started to go down the trail and she whispered to me, "I feel like somebody is watching us."

After being in the service, there's one thing I've learned over a period. That is when you take someone into an area that you've been in and they've never been before, they will get kind of a creepy feeling. I guess it's a human nature type thing in an area that's not familiar to the person.

When she told me this, I said to myself, *"Don't tell her anything or say anything crazy that's going to spook her out of here."*

I went on down about 20-30 feet and it felt like somebody straight up punched me in the guts. I felt my stomach knot up and start hurting. I didn't say anything to Dawn, but from that point on, I felt it, too. We were being watched.

We went a little further down to the bottom of that hill. As soon as we got down there, we heard three loud, sharp whistles. We stopped.

She asked me, "What is that?"

The whole time she was talking to me and asking me what it was, my gut was absolutely killing me.

I said, "Well, what do you think it is? It's not a bird. It's way too loud for a bird. Just keep watching."

So, she did. The next thing I heard her say was, "WHAT is that?"

Probably 30 yards from us, there it was. It was coal black laying on the side of this hill, trying to hide in the golden colored grass. It stuck out like a sore thumb. It looked like if it stood up, it would have been 7-8 feet tall. But it was laying on its side, taking its hand and laying the grass over a little bit so it could see us.

My wife kept asking, "What is it? What is it?"

I said, "Well, what do you THINK it is?"

I didn't want to tell her. I wanted her to tell me what she was seeing. I didn't want to put an idea into her head in case she was seeing anything different.

Finally, she said, "That is one, isn't it?"

I said, "Yep. That's what you're looking at."

She said, "What do we do?"

I said, "We're going to ease back up the trail."

I thought to myself, *"It's probably not alone. We don't want to pursue this. We don't need to put ourselves in harm's way."*

So, we tried to casually ease back up the trail. We had our backs toward the bigfoot, so we didn't see it move, but it had gotten up and went straight up the hill about 25 feet or so to a big tree there.

We stopped and I turned back around to see if it was still there. It was gone, so I thought, *"Oh, no! Where did it go?"*

We were looking around and Dawn goes, "Who is that?" She was pointing up the hill.

It had gone in behind the tree. It was holding a tree branch with one hand and was leaning over to the side looking around at us. It was watching us.

I thought, *"Okay. Cool."*

I had a little 5X digital zoom camera, and I was doing my best to get some pictures. I learned a hard lesson. Little cheap cameras get little cheap pictures. They pixelate very poorly when you try to enhance or enlarge the photos. I did try to get pictures.

From the time we first saw it to the time we left out of the area was 15-20 minutes that we watched this one bigfoot. It was a beautiful Class A sighting. That was my wife's first time out and she got to experience all of this on her first outing!

We had experienced everything in that area from the juveniles playing to a limb being thrown, tree knocks, footprints, and this Class A sighting.

Not long after that my buddy and I went down and camped out in that same place. We had some activity like tree knocks and we could hear them moving in the woods. The next week-end he decided to go by himself and went down to the same place.

The next day he called me up and said, "Bro – You ain't going to believe this."

Me being an Army veteran and my buddy being a Marine veteran, we are both pretty used to being out in the field and knowing how to take care of ourselves. He's one of the kind of guys that it really takes a lot to get him going. It takes a lot to stir him up. When he called me, he was off the charts!

He said, "You ain't going to believe this. I went right back to the same campsite where we were just at last week-end. Everything was good. I had my campfire going. Tent set up. No problem. So, I crawled in the tent, got in my sleeping bag, and closed the tent up."

I could tell this was the part coming up that he thought I might not believe.

"In just a few minutes I heard something moving outside the tent. I was laying there listening to it. First, I thought it was the property owner who gave us permission to be there. Then I started listening and realized there were two of whatever it was out there. One was within just a few feet of the tent. It was walking around the outside of the tent."

He hesitated.

"It was talking. It and the other one that was out there were talking to each other back and forth."

I said, "What do you mean by 'talking'? You're going to have to explain this."

He said, "Do you remember that real abrupt German kind of sound, real gruff?"

I said, "Yeah."

He said, "Well, that's what it sounded like… like an angry German. I couldn't make out a word it was saying, but clearly, it was having a conversation with the other one that was out there."

He said it sounded big based on the volume and the sound of its talking. My buddy was so scared, he wouldn't get out of his tent. Instead he got his two side arms ready that he had with him in case he came under attack.

"If that tent would have moved, it would have been on. It never touched the tent. It never tried to bother me, but I sure wasn't coming out of there! It circled for quite a while, and finally I could hear them both walking off."

That's the spot where I wish we could get back to. It may have changed now because we haven't been in there in a few years. It was really a hot spot from the very first time I ever went in there.

I've been going over to a couple of the state forests. Yellow Wood and Morgan Monroe. I had been out in the woods doing parabolic work, trying to listen to everything. I went back to my camp site and threw my sleeping bag in the back of the truck. I climbed back there and closed the lid down.

I had just laid down and I had a weird feeling that I needed to look out. I opened my eyes and raised my head up a little bit. I had a bigfoot come right up to the truck! Low and behold, there stood a bigfoot at the back of my truck, leaned down, looking in the back end of my truck.

I'm like, *"You've got to be kidding me! I've been over there in the woods all that time, and you wait until I get back here to show up! Seriously?"*

I raised up a little and wanted to see it. It stood straight up. I can't say how tall, but I know it was huge. It turned and walked off. I really wanted to get a good look at it because it was so big.

Another time a bigfoot followed me back to the campsite and stayed right outside the edge of the firelight. It walked all the way around the camp. It never tried to bother me. It stayed right there close and I finally went to bed. I don't know how long it hung out.

There have been so many things that have happened in the last 8-9 years that have really been off the charts. Everything.

I took my wife down to Yellow Wood State Forest at the beginning of this year in early spring to one of the spots where I like to set up. She got out of the truck.

She was like, "You need to come and look at this."

I went over there to see what she was looking at. It was an enormous footprint. I hadn't brought my casting stuff with me that trip. We measured it from the tip of the toe to the heel was 23 inches! It measured 9 inches across at the widest part.

I was like, "You've got to be kidding me! The day I leave my plaster and stuff at home is the day we find this enormous footprint?"

If anybody says that bigfoot doesn't exist in Indiana, I've got news for them! They're wrong. I've seen them, experienced them.

Recently I was talking to a friend of mine who has been into this bigfoot field research for quite a while.

I asked him about people making the calls and doing the wood knocks and stuff, trying to get a response from a bigfoot.

He said, "That's not what they like."

I asked, "What DO they like?"

He said, "Just talk to them. Talk to them like they're people."

He told me to watch him and see what he did, and he'd show me. He went out and started talking into the woods at night. And they would come in. You could see the eyeshine.

We've seen eyeshine in the colors of red, white, and almost a hazy amber color, to green. I've seen the red, and I've seen the white eyes a lot.

One time I was out on my own and I thought about what my friend had said about talking to them. I thought, *"I'm going to try this."*

It worked.

One time I had some people out with me at one of the state forests. One guy in my group was with me and some people from another group were out there. Then we had a family that just showed up who wasn't involved with either one of our groups.

We were sitting around and talking until it got kind of late. One guy had tried doing some howls or whoops. He got no response.

He said, "I'm going to go ahead and go. Usually when I leave, that's when they start showing up and stuff happens!"

Sure enough, about 20 minutes or so after he left, I told the group, "Let me try my technique." So, I got up, went out to the edge of the woods, and started talking to them.

Directly I had one set of white eyes that came in close. One set of red eyes came close. Thirty or 40 feet out, one sat down and was just kind of watching me. I thought maybe the eyeshine closest to the ground might have been from younger ones.

They were playfully throwing rocks. It was as if they were throwing rocks at us underhanded. They weren't trying to hurt us or anything. They were just being kind of playful. It was like, "Here you go… catch this."

This went on for a while. I decided to go to another part of the camping area and check it out. I went around the vehicles and started talking into the woods again. I suddenly realized there was one standing about 10 feet away from me. He was probably somewhere around the 8-foot range. He had the red eyes going on.

I kept talking. "We're not here to hurt you or anything."

The people sitting behind the vehicles started calling me to come and look at something. It was too late. I didn't see anything, but they told me they had seen two silhouettes walk out across the field.

Talking to them works. It draws them in.

Lately we haven't been getting as much activity as we were getting in the past. I'm not sure if there's a migration thing going on and they've left before cold weather or what. I don't know.

I'm still in the learning process of all of this.

Sometimes you can smell them before you see them. They have a stink. Some of them smell like nasty, rotten garbage right up in the middle of the summer. Sometimes they smell musky. It is BAD. The smell will just about make you sick at times.

We don't want to go out into the woods and assume that these creatures are warm, fuzzy things. Although they seem peaceful, I'm sure there's some that could be very mean and aggressive. They are wild creatures, and we must show them some respect. I always give them all the room they need.

I decided to start the Bigfooting Indiana Group mainly because I wanted to get a page going on Facebook and kind of get my story out there. I wanted to find people who had interesting experiences to talk to about the whole thing. I really wasn't shooting for anything big.

The next thing I know I've got a lot of people starting to come into the page. That's when I decided to start a group and see what we can do. I finally got Bigfooting Indiana together.

We've been really blessed. For a long time, we only had about 200 people and now we're over 1,000. I've barely had this thing going for about two years and it's really taken off. It grew that quickly.

Allen Pemberton is one of our admins and Aaron MacIntee is my tech guy. He does audio and video.

We're working on getting a YouTube channel put together where we can start putting more Bigfooting Indiana videos out on YouTube. Aaron got us set up on etsy where people can get our merchandise like hats, hoodies, and t-shirts.

There are a lot of good people in the group, and I've met a lot of good people. I feel very fortunate to have what we have right now. The group is open to anybody who would like to join. If they want to come in, they just need to go to the page, click on join, and we'll put them in.

Sometimes I have people get in touch with me who want to tell me their story. At other times I'll have people get hold of me to tell me about places they have where they've had sightings. They want me to come out and do some investigation work. I have no trouble doing that.

I go anywhere in the state of Indiana. If anyone wants me to come, all they must do is send me a private message and we'll work out the details.

One thing I try to stress to people if I do go somewhere to investigate a sighting is that if they do not want their name used or their location revealed, that's not a problem. I respect everybody's privacy. I don't ever tell my exact locations.

I've gotten some good stories. I had a lady in the northern end of the state who contacted me and was kind of quizzing me about the page. She finally said she had seen some tree structures like the photos she'd seen. She sent pictures and I was very impressed. There's something going on up there.

In the part of the year when there's a lot of activity in an area with suspected bigfoot, I may go out every week-end. I try to get out as much as I can. If anyone has a spot they really want to have me investigate, I will try to go. They can contact me privately through the page and we can work out details.

Two Boys on the Way to the School Bus
Stanley Smith

I've heard that two of the Smith boys in our community saw a bigfoot. Larry Smith, their dad, is the one who told me about it. They were walking out of their holler on the way to meet the school bus early in the morning. They were right where Pea Pace's old place used to be before they put all the other houses, trailers, and stuff in there. Pea Pace used to have two houses that sat right there.

The boys had gotten about halfway from Larry's house to Pea's place. They said something came up out of that bottom and landed right there by the Pace place.

They said it came running out of that big field and stopped and looked at them where they had been walking on the edge of the road. They said it jumped from the edge of the road clean up on the bank on the other side of the road and took off running up through there.

When they got home, they told Larry about it. One of the boys said, "Dad! It looked like a big old gorilla or something!"

He didn't doubt that they had seen something by the way they were telling him about it. He just couldn't figure out what it was but felt sure it wasn't a gorilla like they thought it was.

This happened quite a few years ago and I'm not sure that anybody around here knew about bigfoot at that time. I doubt it they did.

Larry kind of laughed it off. He said to himself, *"I'm going to go down there and see for myself if I see anything like what they're talking about."*

Sammy took his dad down there and showed him the spot where they'd seen the big gorilla looking creature. They looked around in the edge of the field and the road.

Larry said that sure enough, there were tracks around there. Big tracks. Big human type tracks. And where it had jumped up on the side of the hill, its footprints had sunk up in the mud and leaves. He could see the tracks where it had gone right on up into the mountains, just like the boys had told him.

That happened many years ago, long before they started talking about bigfoot on TV or having shows about it. As far as I know, none of them ever saw the creature again after that.

Monkeys Eyebrow
Judith Victoria Hensley

What's in a name? Monkeys Eyebrow in McCreary County, Kentucky has long puzzled me. Why in the world would anybody name a place Monkey's Eyebrow?

I saw my first black panther there back in the mid-1970s with Elmer and Irene Boggs. So, the name and the experience has always stuck with me along with the curiosity about the name.

When I posted a picture on Facebook with the name, I was happy to get the following response from Karen Smith Byers.

"The story my grandpa always told about Monkey's Eyebrow was interesting. He said when the first settlers came into that area, there was a tribe of hairy men resembling monkeys who lived there.

They supposedly swung through the trees and threw rocks at the settlers to run them off. Their faces were human-like, and they had huge eyes and thick eyebrows.

Hence the name."

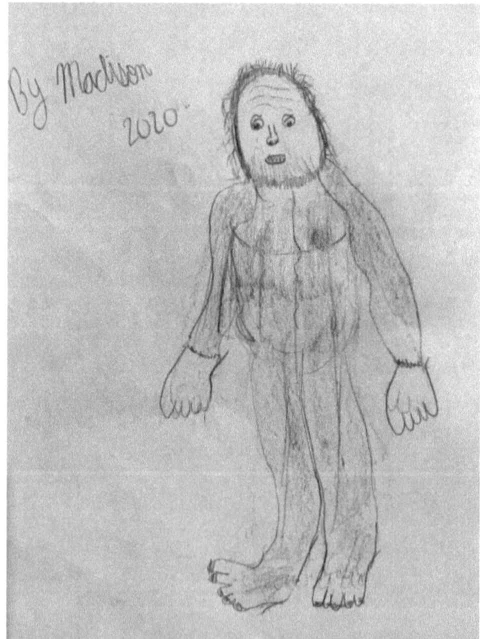

Original Artwork by Madison Correll

Was It Bigfoot?
Frankie Mobelini

I've never seen a bigfoot, but I might have heard one.

I used to make fun of the blasting calls they'd feature on *Finding Bigfoot*. I've been in the woods and learned to hunt from the time I was about four years old and nobody I know has ever seen or heard anything like that. I'm 44 years old and I've seen and heard many things over the years.

My wife, daughter, and I had been fishing on the North Fork of the Kentucky River. We hadn't heard anything all night. By the time the catfish started biting good my six-year old daughter had already got into the tent and fell asleep on our air mattress.

The time was around 1:00 a.m. or a little after, the dogs started barking, coyotes started yelping, house cats started screaming, and wild cats started screaming!

I told Lori, "That's the strangest thing!"

She said, What is that?"

I explained to her that usually every animal in the woods wild or domestic doesn't turn on at the same time.

That's when I heard the thing I've never heard before or since in the woods. It was a deep roar like noise, but not exactly that. Everything in the woods stopped making any noise at all. Then the scream/roar came again and was louder!

I've heard whitetail bucks in rut sound like a red stag from Europe, but most people didn't believe that happens either until I took a few guys hunting with me and they heard it for themselves.

I unholstered a .44-40 8-inch revolver. I didn't know what in the world was out there or if it was a danger to my family, but there's not much if anything in the woods I'd be afraid that a .44-40 wouldn't put down.

We were worried that whatever it was would step out of the woods and be headed toward us. Not being able to identify the sound was the scariest part. It had to be within 15-20 yards (maximum) of us. We knew this because up a small hill and across on open bottom to a thicket, were the railroad tracks.

It sounded like a huge primate. That's the only way my friend Clint and I could explain it. It sounded similar to the blasting calls on the television series *Finding Bigfoot* that I used to make fun of.

I will probably never know for sure what it was. As far as making fun of bigfoot stuff - I don't do that anymore!

From Skeptic to Researcher
Taylor Cook (Squatch Watchers)

I was a pure skeptic when I first heard about people telling their bigfoot encounters. When I was a kid, I'd get my mother to tell me bigfoot stories, as well as my uncles. They'd tell me about encounters they'd had with bigfoot. As a kid, I didn't take them for the truth. I just thought they were made up stories.

I was about twenty years old when all this first captured my attention, and that was about nine years ago.

My friend David invited me to go out with him on one of his field research jaunts in the woods looking for any sign of bigfoot. I went along for the fun of it, still skeptical about the whole thing.

David said, "Let me give out a call."

He did that and all the animals were still going crazy making noises in the background. Some creature answered him with a loud yell. When it did, it silenced everything else in the woods. Dead silence.

We kind of got addicted to making the calls and hoping for an answer right then. But since we didn't see anything, I wasn't convinced about it all. We heard stuff. We heard cracks and pops in the woods that were unusual. We saw signs of something big being in the woods. We saw a few tracks that were unusual.

Three years later, I was still a skeptic. David took me back to a place that was one way in, one way out. It was at least a mile or mile and a half in on private property. We got to the spot and went our own way from there.

Tate Fulbright, David Martin, Taylor Cook

This is what turned me from being a skeptic to a believer in one night.

We were out there interacting with a rock formation. Now, I know some people will say that sounds crazy, but a big rock would show up in the middle of a trail where there hadn't been a big rock before. And rocks would be stacked on top of each other.

David stacked some up his own way. We went back the next week and David noticed that it looked like the rocks had been kicked over and scattered out. Big rocks kicked uphill and spread out would have had to have a lot of force to do that. We were filming it and telling the local TV producer, Rex, who does a local show, about it.

The phone rang and suddenly this big boulder comes flying through the air and lands right behind me! That's the point when I knew for sure there was something else out there with us. It had to be big and it had to be able to throw a big rock. I wasn't a skeptic anymore. Whatever animal threw that rock had to have hands to pick it up and hurl it at us!

Taylor Cook

All of this is on one of our YouTube videos. We uploaded all this stuff to a local TV network, WHKY.

We continued our search. One time we decided to throw apples out through the woods. Something started tossing them back. Again, whatever it was had to have hands to pick up and throw accurately back in our direction, but we never saw who or what was doing it.

Right before we walked out of the woods we heard this big noise – loud, and rolling like a cross between a grunt, a growl, and a roar.

I locked myself in the car that night. Not David. He went charging after it in the direction it came from. He wants to be the first guy to get a bigfoot bruise!

I was locked in the car and we had all these flashlights with us. That's when David had his first Class One sighting. He was featured on *Animal Planet*. He saw this thing lean out, look at him, and then lean back in behind the trees and he didn't see it again.

The next day we went back in the daylight. There was a footprint and break away up in the tree about eight feet up where it looked like the creature had twisted the limb up so he could maybe see around the tree.

Tate in the front Taylor in the back strange stick stuck in the ground.

We were the first two officially to become a team dedicated to doing bigfoot research in the area. About three years later, Tate Fulbright joined our team.

I had told him stories about our adventures for years. He said, "Man, you're crazy! There's other people out in the woods playing tricks on you!"

I said, "No. We hear stuff. We see stuff. It's all true. Come on and go with us."

He was a major skeptic at the time. So, he came with us and witnessed the rock throwing for himself. Something was throwing rocks at him.

David beside a structure.

He said, "Wow! There really was something throwing rocks at me and I can't explain it." That's when he got addicted to finding answers and joined the team.

We have a YouTube video called *The Bigfoot Tunnel System*.

It happened where Tate had his first sighting on the same property. At this point we've had three sightings on that property.

When Tate had his sighting, he watched this thing go down into a gulley. He saw the shoulders and the head. He said it was a gray color.

We went back with him the next day and there was like a canopy of trees interwoven that stretched out for about the length of two football fields, forming a tunnel. All that's on video on our YouTube channel.

On the same property, there's a wedding venue. People at a wedding have claimed to see something hairy step off into the woods.

We often hear what is known as "the wild man chatter" between the creatures. It IS wild. It sounds like primate noise back and forth. We believe there is a community of bigfoot living there.

Because of the videos and images we've posted we've caught the interest of a couple of NFL players. They contacted us and wanted to go with us into the woods. We were happy to take them.

The day they were with us, we found a couple of size 18-inch prints on a sand bed. We took video of it. They got to witness the "yelling," also.

There was a lot of noise in the woods and coyotes going wild. David let out one of his yells and everything was still going nuts. Suddenly we hear the yell of what we think is a bigfoot. It silenced EVERYTHING, even the coyotes. Anyone that's been around coyotes knows that they don't shut up for anything unless something dominant shows up. They had been going crazy, then fell completely silent when they heard the yell of the creature that responded to David.

DeAngelo Williams and Gary Barnidge can vouch for this. They're on video. They started out as pure skeptics, just curious. Dee even brought his $3,000 night scope that he takes hog hunting.

One of the weird things that often happens around a bigfoot sighting is that battery charges go completely dead. That happens a lot. When we start getting bigfoot activity out in the woods, our cameras, cell phones, and other equipment often lose power. They go from full charge in preparation for a trip into the woods, to completely dead.

We can't explain how this happens or why.

At this point we feel like we've developed some kind of relationship with them. Actually – we feel like we have become a source of entertainment for them.

No, we don't go speak to them or get to talk to them or pet them or anything like that. But they know when we're there and we kind of know when they're there.

Sometimes they follow us to our base camp. One time something pushed over a dead tree to get our attention. They've also thrown rocks on top of the tin building there. It's crazy.

Toby doing a tree knock.

Everyone we take out with us is a skeptic on some level to start with, like the two NFL players. But then they saw the footprints, started hearing things, and heard something big splash into the water in the creek. It means so much to us when people go with us and experience part of what we experience, then believe there is something going on out there.

That kind of thing is important to us. I mean, we don't get paid for doing this or the amount of time we spend in the woods.

We're spending that time away from our families. It is addicting when we feel like we might be getting close to some answers. It's fun when a skeptic comes along and then begins to reconsider.

All our stuff is documented.

Our friend Toby Bolick was a pure skeptic.

One night, Toby (who has since become another team member), David, and I were out. We had been hearing the "wildman chatter." David slipped off the golf cart and he swears up and down to this. He said that two creatures walked right up beside of him doing the "chatter talk."

He says that's the most scared he's ever been in his whole life. He started rustling and letting them know he was there. Then the two creatures ran off.

All of this has happened on the same property in western North Carolina. We never betray the exact location. The owner is a great guy, but he doesn't want his location out to the public for general knowledge.

Tim Peeler was featured on Jay Leno after he had a bigfoot sighting. He didn't get a cast of the print. One week prior to his sighting, our team got a print about five miles away (as the crow flies) from his sighting location in a straight line to his property. We believe our cast of the print to be one of the best casts made of a bigfoot print in North America. It was made in North Carolina. That was a motivating factor for us.

We just want to get to the bottom of, "What IS in North Carolina?"

We believe there is a community of sasquatch in North Carolina. We've found baby prints that have been casted with pictures taken. There have been multiple sightings in our state, print casts, and many unexplainable incidents.

Taylor showing how tall the structure is. He is 5'11".

We meet a lot of people in a lot of places who have experienced similar things to what we have. We go to different states to conferences or to places people invite us to do investigations.

One unusual question that we've been asked several times is, "Have you seen the lights?" Yes, we have. They will make cold chills run up your body.

The first time my wife, (then my fiancée, Paige Park) went with us on a field event, no one had mentioned anything to her about lights. When we take a person with us for the first time, we don't tell them what to look for or what to expect. We want to hear from them what they are seeing or hearing for the very first time. We don't feed people information or condition them about what might happen.

We tell them, "Tell us what you see."

They might study our videos before they come or watch other shows about bigfoot, but we never precondition them to anything.

The first time Paige was with us, she witnessed the flash of green light, and then the activity started. This doesn't happen every single time, but we've had so many people who say they have seen it.

She said, "I just saw a GREEN flash of light!"

I didn't give her a clue. I just said, "Really?"

Then she started hearing the breaks, twig snaps. She had a piece of twig thrown at her. Afterwards we told her about the other people who had talked about seeing the green light flash before bigfoot activity on our videos. Now, she's a believer.

She and I had a Class A sighting together. This was about a week after DeAngelo Williams and Gary Barnidge had been out with us. We had left David in the woods by himself near where we found the big 18-inch footprint. Before we left, I handed him my gun.

"Here. Take this for protection. It's not for protection against a bigfoot, but for any other animal out here that might attack you." We take bear mace to use and other stuff, just in case we come up on something at the wrong time and startle it or get too close to cubs.

Paige said, "I really hate to leave him out there by himself!"

She paused, then added, "I'm not afraid of the animals out here. I'm afraid of PEOPLE, like this crazy guy walking across the road!"

As soon as she said, "walking across the road," I looked up.

"HOLY COW!" she said.

The creature was probably not full grown. It was only about six feet tall. Then she saw the glowing eyes.

She said, "THAT'S NOT anybody!"

I said, "No, it's not!"

We went back in to tell David. "Hey, there was something that just ran across the road up here."

We picked him up and drove back to the spot. We got out of the car and there was grass laid down from whatever had run across the road.

That was what we believe was her first sighting of sasquatch that night.

It was solid black, up on two feet. It cleared a two-lane highway in about three giant strides. It was "Boom! Boom! Boom!" and on the other side into the grass. It was really moving.

Until that night she was a pure skeptic. She's asked me, "WHY do you waste your time on this stuff? Why do you go to these conferences?"

Now she knows.

It Let Me Live
Ricky Sexton

Here's my story. It's not just a story. It's true. It's what really happened to me and it's up to every individual person to decide whether they believe it or not, but a man knows what he knows. A man knows what he saw!

It was the early 1990s. I was blasting for Nally and Hamilton Enterprises in the head of Leatherwood at a place called Guthrie Branch Blue Diamond Coal Company. It mined out years and years ago, I think in the 1940s. We were contour stripping that site.

It was a hot clear sunny day. My brother, James, and I were on the drill bench waiting for the driller to get some holes drilled so we could load them for blasting. James (we always called him Bo) worked with me on the blasting crew.

While we were waiting, our boss came up and said, "I've got some permit signs that need to be put up when you have time to get it done."

So, while we were waiting on the drill we decided to go and put them up. The signs must be placed above where they're going to stop stripping and below where the process started.

Bo said, "I'll take the top and you can get the bottom."

I took off and was putting up a sign about every 100 feet apart. After putting up several signs I was quite a way out into the woods. As I was walking along I saw some bushes shaking a little up ahead of me on the side of the hill. It was sloped a little.

I thought, *"That's Bo. He's got his signs up and he's coming down where I'm at."*

I hollered at him about three times, but he never answered. I just kept walking and when I got to where the bushes had been shaking I looked and all I saw was a big ball of brown hair.

My thought was, *"This is a bear!"*

I was getting nervous. I had no gun. All I had with me was a homemade hammer, a few permit signs, and a pocket full of nails. Then I thought to myself, *"If this were a bear it would be black! There's no brown bears here!"*

About that time that brown ball of fur raised its head up and I knew that it definitely was not a bear! A bear has a snout like a dog. This thing's face was as flat as a human being's face.

I was standing there wondering, *"What in the world am I looking at?"*

I was so nervous, but I was trying to be as still as I could. I'm was no more than twenty feet in front of this thing. It sat there on the side of the hill while I watched it. It had two big arms in front of it holding itself up. I was staring right in the face of this thing, afraid to move.

When it looked at me it was like it looked past me. It didn't look into my eyes but like it was looking past my head, off to the side. Then it stuck it's face up in the air like a dog does when it's winding something. I knew then it smelled something and hoped it wasn't me.

I thought, *"Oh, God! This thing smells me! This is how I'm going to die! This thing is going to kill me and eat me right here in these woods!"*

I was shaking like a leaf! I was only about twenty feet in front of this creature. About that time its bottom lip curled out like it turned inside out. I could see the pink part of its mouth and those big teeth.

I freaked out! I shot out of there like a rocket. I honestly thought I was going to die. There was no way I could have fought this thing and no way I could outrun it. This creature was built like *The Hulk* - nothing but muscle hair and teeth!

As I ran through the woods I was afraid to look behind me. I was afraid I would see it coming after me! I didn't want to see that. I would rather it come up behind me and take me out suddenly than for me to see it coming with no way to stop it. What few times I did look, I never saw it behind me. It didn't follow me that I could tell.

It's a wonder I didn't run into a tree when I did look behind me because I definitely didn't stop. I kept running. It didn't bother me. If it had wanted to, it could have killed me very easily and very quickly. It let me live and I respect it for that.

There are two things about that day I will never ever forget. Those big teeth and those eyes are imprinted in my mind. That thing's eyes were as black as coal. The closest I can come to comparing what I saw with any other creature I've ever seen is a big gorilla.

I never saw it stand up but with its flat nose and it's kind of pointed head like a gorilla's, it's is the closest thing I can find that would look like that creature.

I learned to never tell a bunch of guys you work with a story like that. They ran me in the ground over it, but all in good fun. They liked to joke about it.

Some of the guys on the night shift said they had talked to some older people who lived in that hollow years and years ago before we strip mined it. They were told that there was always something unexplained that was seen there.

That's my story. It's a true story. I don't know what it was or where it came from or if it's still there. All I know for a fact is that on a certain day, at a certain time, that creature and I were no more than twenty feet apart in front of each other.

It let me live.

Original Artwork by Nadia Martinez

Bigfoot Watcher in the Woods
Rosemary Johnson

I live in Black Mountain, Kentucky in Harlan County. It is a very large county and a lot of it is wilderness land. Last year at the end of the summer, my boyfriend, Donnie Blevins, and I went ginsenging. We went as far back as we could go in his truck up into Black Mountain. We parked the truck and were making our way up the mountain on foot.

We got up to the place we wanted to start. There were ridges up above us. We hadn't made our way to the top or even the middle yet. We were walking and looking for ginseng. Donnie decided to go on ahead of me a little way and I stayed where I was and continued looking for ginseng. We could cover more ground if we looked separately.

Suddenly I heard a noise.

Where we were located, no four-wheelers or anybody could have gotten up there. I'm pretty sure of that. It was just the two of us. I kept hearing branches breaking.

I looked up to the left of where I was, in the direction that the noise had come from. It's not like the branches breaking were little things. The sound was from big ones being broken.

I know there are bears in the mountains around here, but I was pretty sure a bear walking through the woods could not make the loud sounds of branches breaking that I was hearing. If a bear did break a branch just by passing through the undergrowth, it wouldn't be that loud.

The noises sounded deliberate. Then I could hear what sounded like stomping. What came to my mind was "bigfoot," but I hadn't seen him at that point.

It seemed like whatever it was got irritated by us being there. Then rocks started being thrown. Bears don't do that. They also don't stomp on purpose when they walk. The big branch breaks continued. It was nothing I had ever experienced being up in the mountains before that day.

The creature's behavior toward me was very pronounced. It seemed like it was trying to scare me out of the mountains. It made sure I heard it breaking branches.

I had the feeling like, *"Something knows I'm here. It doesn't want me here."* That's the kind of feeling that I got from it, that it wanted me to leave.

I kept looking up at that ridge where I heard all the noise coming from. I saw something black, all black, standing there. I couldn't make out much. It was no bear. It was like the figure of a man.

It felt like it was saying to me, *"Hey! I know you're here, and I'm making myself be known to you. It's time for you to get out of here."*

It was throwing its little fit making sure I knew it was up there.

I told myself, *"We've just gotten started. Maybe my imagination is playing tricks. I'm not going to let myself get scared up and make us have to leave when we barely got up here. It's too hard and too far to have to come back later."*

I made my way to where my boyfriend was and started telling him about it. I don't know if he believed it or not. He said, "Well, let's go on up here a bit and if we don't find any ginseng soon, we'll just go back out."

We might have gone another two miles deeper into the mountain. We were there a couple more hours before we decided to leave. We made our way back down to where I saw the bigfoot. We didn't hear another thing.

I don't know why I did it, but dumb old me started making the whooping sounds that they make. I guess I wanted to see if one would call back. I guess I wanted to prove to Donnie that I really had seen one. If there's one around and a person makes that whooping sound, they might call back, or start throwing rocks at the person.

I don't know if that sound is the mating call they do or what. Then Donnie started doing it.

Suddenly I thought, *"How DUMB is this? What are we doing trying to call them in???"* Not a little more than two hours earlier I had the experience of seeing one for myself. I didn't want to see it again!

We decided we'd better quit making those noises and quit trying to call one in. We never did hear an answer.

Where I live in Black Mountain, it's not very congested. I live a good way up in here.

I don't have many neighbors. I do have some, but they're not close, though. I have almost an acre to myself. There are mountains all around me. There's a creek that flows through.

This summer I heard something, and my cousin said he heard it, too. It was about 1:00 o'clock in the morning. I was sitting out in my yard looking up at the night sky. I love to do that in the summer – just sit out on a warm night and look at the stars.

I heard a holler like something I'd never heard before. It sounded like something between a man and a beast. I know there are panthers in these mountains, and I know their screams. It was nothing like them.

It was a very loud, "Aaaaaaaaaaarrrrrrrr!" between a holler and a growl. It wasn't from a man. I know that. Some people say that's the sound when it's bigfoot.

I know there are things up here in these mountains, especially up there where I had that experience last year ginsenging. It was like it wanted to make sure that I knew he was saying, *"Hey! I know you're up here. Get out!"*

It was very strange. There are things in these mountains that we just don't understand.

Georgia Museum Chronicles Reports from
Eyewitnesses (printed with Permission)
Dave Bakara
(Expedition Bigfoot)

Skunk "ape" sighting!

I spoke with a very reliable witness last night. He had an interesting sighting three years ago headed to his office on Florida's east coast. He was driving north on 29, in route to I-75, when he observed what he thought was a bear alongside of the left shoulder of the road. As he approached, this bear stood up to a height of 7-8 feet, rusty brown in color.

He said it took two steps and leapt off its left foot and cleared the wildlife retaining fence that was right behind it. He said he had no idea how it could easily clear such a high fence. The wildlife fences along I-10 in Florida are 10' tall. He said this fence was at least 8' and thinks it may have had a barbed wire slope on top of that! Two steps and an impossible leap. I've heard this many, many times. Artwork credit: Michael Montoya.

Tractor Mower Incident

Aug 28th, 2018. Cut Off, Louisiana.

A nice man came to the museum today. He spent a long time looking and listening to everything. When he came out, he told us a great story that happened to his friend and neighbor of MANY years.

His friend was on a tractor cutting grass at about 10:00 a.m. on a large parcel of land. It bordered a pasture, and the shape of the property required him to drive his tractor alongside a canal that separated the pastureland from the miles of marshland. He made a left turn along the canal and right in front of him stood a very wide, hairy man. He said it was squatted down a little but couldn't have been much taller than him (5'10"). Though its knees were bent a little, he said it was the width and power he noticed immediately.

He locked eyes with this creature for about 12 seconds, then it turned and began to run off towards the marsh. He said he's never seen anything move that fast in his life. For the life of him, he could not understand how something built like that, could run so fast.

He said as it ran, its feet were swinging behind it as high as its shoulders. And the feet were thick padded, and almost a white/dull gray color. He said this thing could easily run down a deer.

He described the face as looking exactly like a man, black skin, but with dark hair all over, except under the eyes and around the nose. He said it had a look of sheer terror on its face. He said it looked like it was shaking in fear as it locked eyes with him. He told his neighbor (the man I met), and his neighbor returned with him the next day. They found tracks where it was standing and packed down grass where it must have been sleeping before it was awakened by the tractor/mower.

Smoker Incident

A nice man came in today and donated original casts taken from Ocoee, Tennessee last year. A woman was watching/stoking a smoker with a whole turkey, on the back porch of their home. At about 10:00 a.m. she had just added chips and knew the smoker was at 270°.

As she continued her housework, she heard her little dog barking at an alarming pitch. She rounded the hall and glanced at the sliding glass door to the smoker and saw that a huge hairy brown creature was now standing on the porch with its back to her. It seemed to be leaning over the smoker. It slowly turned his head and shoulders toward her, then spun around again, and began to scream in pain, VERY LOUD.

It jumped over the railing to the ground below and was gone. She then saw the lid off the smoker and realized it had picked up the hot smoker with intentions of carrying it off...the next day the crew working on the porch extension found this handprint in a pile of dry mortar where it had slipped and fell at the bottom of the porch.

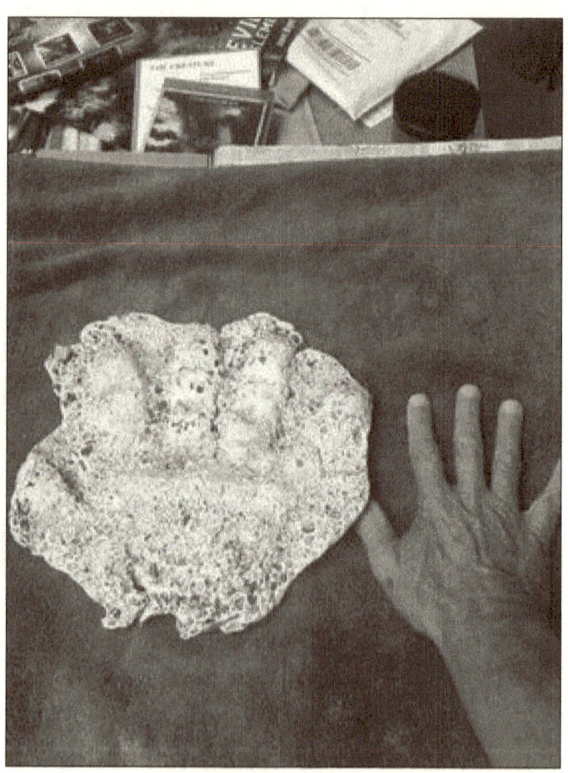

This summer, the family noticed cabbages and beets being pulled up at the far edge of the garden, nearest the woods. Her son discovered this footprint in the tilled soil/ He cast it and donated them both to the museum. ~EB

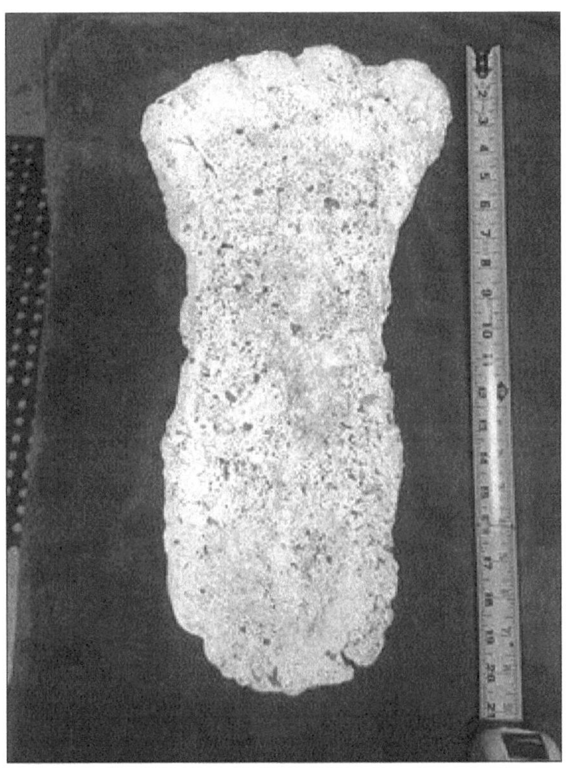

Ape-Man

Bigfoot sighting in Blue Ridge, Georgia one week ago.

A woman came to tell us she observed a very large ape-man walk through her back property. She saw through her living room window as it came across her long driveway at approximately 8:00 p.m. It then walked down towards her small creek, and she ran to her other window.

Through that window she observed it walking along the edge of the creek for a short distance. It then turned a hard left and walked straight up the steep hill behind her house.

She said it was huge, was dark brown, and walked fully erect. The pointed head sat on very wide shoulders, at a slightly forward tilt as it walked.

She said it did not seem to be in any hurry. She knows it will eventually be back... and she will be waiting, ~EB

Law Enforcement Officer

I had a fascinating conversation with a law enforcement officer today. He had an up close and personal encounter while hunting. I will not divulge which state or city. He was hunting in a regional, mountain WMA, sitting quietly in his deer stand at 11:30 am. He was approximately 35 feet up in a climbing stand.

He could hear something walking in his direction. It was big and not quiet. It wasn't until it was almost underneath him that he could see it. It stopped 15 feet from the base of his tree. He was gobsmacked by what he was looking at.

This creature was massive. It was very broad at the shoulders, with huge arms. He said he didn't know why, but he had sprayed apple scent on himself, and it looked right up at him. He said he thought he was *"looking into the eyes of the devil"* (he has since realized it had no evil intent).

He locked eyes with it, and he knew, *"This creature could have scaled that tree and put one hand over me and squeezed me like a pimple."*

After it looked up at him, it let out a small snort, turned, and with no great hurry, walked off into the woods. He said this creature walked with a confident swagger like it knew nothing could hurt it. It WAS the boss. He heard it walk into the woods, then it stopped.

Still frightened, he waited till 5:00 p.m. before climbing down and leaving, but was concerned it was still there, waiting. ~EB

Turkey Hunter's Story

This man showed me a photo of a beautiful footprint on his camera today in the museum.

He was turkey hunting solo in the Green Swamp three years ago. He had his back to a tree and was using his turkey call. He had a great view of a small opening.

As he was sitting against a tree, completely covered in camo, he heard something walking up behind him. It was something big and definitely on two feet. As it approached directly behind the tree it stopped. Then from the edge of the clearing ahead, he heard a clear "whoop." Whatever this thing was behind him answered back in the same "WHOOOOP" sound.

He was completely freaked out and had to see what this was. As he turned to see, it exploded in leaves and twigs and was gone in the blink of an eye. It was gone unnaturally fast. He could hear it crashing into the woods, and huge splashes as it ran thru the swamp.

He said he knew he had a 12-gauge shotgun, so his fear was subsided. He decided to try and track it. But after a very short distance, he realized this thing ran thru water that was up to his waist. He decided to turn around and cancel his hunt.

Turkey Hunting Guide into the Green Swamp

A man from Florida came in the museum today. He's a turkey hunting guide from central Florida. He guides hunts into the Green Swamp. Told me his and his dad's story.

His dad worked for a concrete company in the 1960's. He was servicing a machine at a Florida Forestry fire tower under construction near St Cloud. It was in a heavily wooded area at the end of a narrow forest service road. The tower and outbuilding were inside a large fenced, graded area.

He heard a commotion outside the fence as he worked and walked out from under the machinery to see who was out there in this remoteness. He observed three large, upright walking apes making their way along the fence line. Yes, THREE!

He told his son, a few family members, and took this story to the grave with him, never wavering from the facts.

Old Florida Homestead

A 16-year old girl and her mom visited the museum this week and related an encounter from two months ago near Homasassa, Florida.

One Saturday night in April, the mother wanted to show her daughter and her friend her old homestead just 3-4 miles from their house. The mom had heard strange sounds coming from the woods there her whole life.

They were in a pickup truck with the two girls in the bed, backing down a narrow dirt road approaching the old property. A 7-8-foot-tall creature stepped out of the woods and into the road right behind the truck. It stood there as the mother (who did not see it) continued to back down toward it.

The girls described it as huge, standing upright, with long arms almost to its kneecaps, covered in 4" cream colored hair all over. Its eyes reflected the red lights on the back of the truck. When the mom stopped because of all the screaming, the creature took a step toward the truck.

The girls' screaming continued until the mother put the truck in forward, and quickly sped off. As she did, the creature jumped back into the woods in a flash.

The daughter is now hearing strange knocking sounds coming from the woods in back of the house she lives in now, which is only a short drive from her mom's old place. ~EB

Chasing Fireflies

A nice woman and her grown daughter came into the museum yesterday. She was from the Murphy, North Carolina area. She related a short but obviously unsettling story that greatly frightened her when it happened. It has had a negative impact on her life growing up.

When she was a child, on a summer evening, she was chasing fireflies at her home. She was running around her backyard in and out of tall bushes, laughing loudly as she went. As she rounded a stand of small trees, she ran INTO a Bigfoot that must have been watching her. She literally ran right into it.

She looked up at this enormous creature, then ran into her house crying and terrified. Her mother told her it must have been a bear, but this woman insists it was no bear. She's had nightmares her whole life after this about the incident. ~EB

Female Bigfoot

In 1975, a man and his wife were traveling back from attending a funeral in Weber Canyon, Utah. It was very late (near 2:00 a.m.) and his wife was sleeping in the passenger seat.

As he rounded a curve, he noticed what he thought was a girl down on her knees on the side of the road. As he approached her, she stood up and he got a great look at this "girl".

She appeared no more than 5'4" tall, covered in 4" auburn hair all over her body except her face and breasts. He described her as not wide in the hips, though built strong. She looked him right in the eyes as he passed her on the driver's side.

He said his shocked response woke his wife, and he'd traveled a good mile before he realized he should have stopped and approached this creature.

He then added that, though she was beautiful in her own right, she could have easily torn him limb from limb.

I haven't mentioned that he was a police officer at the time. ~EB

Bigfoot to the Rescue

I was 16. It was a hot summer and the rain had been falling off and on for days. My parents owned a bait shop. We sold all types of fishing tackle, and live bait. The rain had stopped for a couple of days, with a forecast of more to follow within the next day.

With buckets in hand myself, my father, and one of my father's friends went out to get catawba worms. The trees were full, and we needed to get to them before the next rain, because we knew the area would soon be flooded and inaccessible.

We split up and began filling our buckets. The ground was soft, and I was afraid of falling in the water. I had seen gators in the area before, especially when the water rose. My bucket was about half full and I was working on a tree close to the bank.

As I made my way around the tree I could feel the ground giving away. I screamed as I began to fall. Someone grabbed me and pulled me up to solid ground. I thought it was my father, but as I looked closer I realized I was wrong. My knees were already weak from the fear of falling but when I saw who grabbed me it was as though I had no legs.

I stood there and could not believe what I was seeing. The creature was huge! The odor was sour and musty.

At first I panicked even more but he made a grunting noise and I felt calm. The feeling was in my chest and I didn't understand what he had done. He stood and looked at me and I looked into the kindliest eyes I had ever seen. He did not move for a few seconds until I heard my father calling my name as he ran to where I was.

Then I saw something that to this day I will never forget. He stepped back into the tree line. As he did his hair began to bristle almost like a cat. As he did this, I saw different shades of hair. It basically camouflaged him, and it was very hard to see him.

My father jumped across the water to the tree I was standing by. I couldn't even speak, I just stood there remembering all the stories I had heard about something big living in the bottoms.

My father helped me get back across the area that had given away to the trail I had walked down earlier. There sat my bucket still half full of worms, and I thought I had dropped it when I fell. I wanted to leave, but I finished filling my bucket because I knew we wouldn't be able to get back in once the rain started again.

On the way home my father said I must have stepped in something because my shirt stank. I wasn't going to say anything to anyone. Who would believe me? As we got out of the truck at the shop I was heading straight to the shower.

My father's friend whispered as I walk by him, "I saw it."

I just kept walking. I still live in the same town and I go back to the area in hopes of seeing him again. Sadly, I haven't. I do, however, leave things to thank him. Maybe one day I will see him again.

I have often wondered what I would do. I live on the Texas, Arkansas line. We were in the bottoms close to Fouke, Arkansas. So, if you ever get down this way, keep your eyes open .

From an original post on *Bigfoot and Dogman Info Library*, with permission from Patricia Adams. (Permission to reprint from David Bakara)

Predator Hunter

Montezuma, Georgia 2017.

A big man came to the museum yesterday. He was about 6'7" and weighed at least 300 pounds. He was a big man by anyone's standards. He told me of his unforgettable trip in Montezuma, Georgia.

He is a predator and problem animal hunter. He was hunting hogs on a property for three consecutive nights. The first two nights, he heard whoops and yells coming from directions all around him. He shrugged it off, not knowing what they were, but remained undeterred.

On the third night, he located the group of problem pigs. He was advancing across a field in their direction 100 yards away. He then heard a very loud howl coming from his left, and he swung his thermal scope to the wood line. He saw a low animal crouched behind a bush and thought at first it was a bear.

Then this creature stood up, and stepped into the open, headed straight for the hogs down a small hill. He said its arm swing left no doubt what he was looking at. It never looked in his direction though he said it had to know he was there.

He wasted no time in getting out of that field, and it's never been far from his mind since then. ~EB

Rose's Report

Dalton, Georgia.1990.

Eighteen-year old "Rose" was driving on Beaverdale Road with her boyfriend (of that time). As they approached the "Y" fork in the road, he slowed the Jeep to bear right.

Out from the woods stepped a huge, upright hairy figure. It stepped out right next to the Jeep, and both she and her boyfriend clearly saw it. It had long hair on the arms and was very tall. After they passed it, her boyfriend was excited and slowed to turn the Jeep around for a second look.

Rose said she beat the heck out his dash and screamed, "Oh no you're not! Take me home right now!" He obliged, and they drove off leaving the "big man" behind. ~EB

Expedition Bigfoot is a 4000 square foot complex with genuine artifacts, life size displays, a mini research vehicle, a full-size Sasquatch model, Florida, and Georgia sighting maps, "Sasquatch Theater" and more!

North Georgia's newest family attraction promises it's a place where entertainment meets education. It is said to have the country's largest permanent display of genuine bigfoot artifacts, life sized exhibits, photos, sketches, large up to date sighting maps, and the World's only Bigfoot Research and Tech Vehicle on display.

Discovering the Truth
Daniel Benoit, Founder and Researcher
East Coast Researchers Organization (E.C.B.R.O.)

Daniel Benoit

As one who grew up in nature as a child playing and hunting with my father, I became quite familiar with wildlife. As the years went by, the thought of bigfoot wasn't anything I dwelt on or thought of, but I had heard of bigfoot and had that information in the back of my mind. It was not until seeing the Roger Patterson and Bob

Gimlin film footage of their bigfoot sighting on the west coast being analyzed by professionals that my curiosity was struck.

From this inspiration, a great interest grew into a strong passion and love for research dedicated to sasquatch. I started off as an independent investigator. Others took notice of my work during the rise of public interest and sightings of sasquatch. The subject was becoming more open and widely known among the public yet was not accepted at the time as truth.

I soon learned after conducting my own research that a much larger community of researchers existed. These individuals were dedicated to the study and discussion of bigfoot. This community was found on social media, hidden from most non-believers and skeptics. It was kept quiet to protect individuals' identities and reputations against the mockery and ridicule of the close minded, the unaware, and those uninterested in discovering the truth.

As an independent investigator, I soon began researching the theories that many had developed which were floating around on the web. I went forward with a very open mind, believing that anything is possible, especially in dealing with the unknown.

My awareness was opened more broadly. My senses were alerted, and I became more in touch with nature as I explored in greater depth the possibility of bigfoot being a real creature. I began to pay special attention to the known wildlife around me. I started noting behaviors and patterns of different animals in an effort to discover how the wildlife lived.

Observation of odd structures associated with the presence of sasquatch became known, and the world around me opened even more. This marked the beginning of my personal discoveries. I developed a passion for wildlife, tracks, habitats, and behavior.

Add to that the discovery of huge unknown humanoid bipedal tracks. Throughout my early field work came many more findings of larger tracks in deeply remote locations along the east coast.

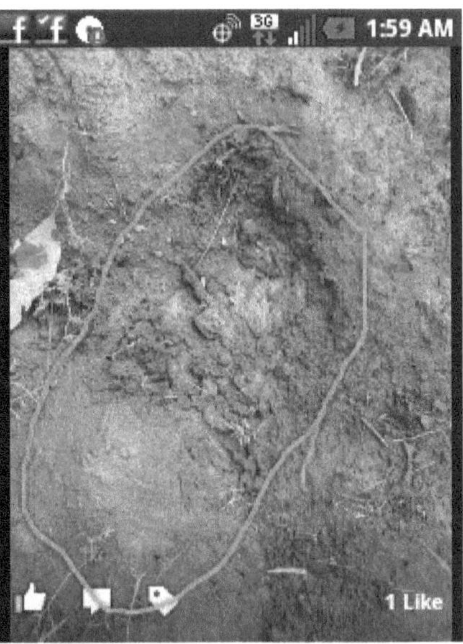

With my senses more keenly developed, and my mind more in tune to the world around me, an awareness of forest sounds was heightened. I took notice of the sounds of all known species around me as well as recognizing various sounds of those unknown.

In preparation for my field research I included studies comparing all known wildlife, both foreign and domestic. The more I studied, I was able to match the known species with their sounds and behaviors.

For example, the great apes are well known by the world. The public is aware of the appearance of these primates. They display behaviors similar to behaviors of the animal we refer to as bigfoot or sasquatch in America. They make long howls for unknown reasons, whoops, and tree knocks.

In the sasquatch world, we all have a lot of theories, but until they are proven, we can't say for sure anything that will convince the scientific community that bigfoot exists. What we can say for sure are our own personal experiences.

I think it's safe to say that sasquatch is in the primate family. Science just hasn't yet figured out which branch of that tree sasquatch belongs on or will shake out of.

My territory in which I do research is so vast, it is a large area to cover. Still, I like small groups. When we spread out for a field research expedition, we can stay in touch with radio communication. If we hear a tree knock or a whoop, we can check with each other and make sure it wasn't coming from another part of our team.

It will take seeing for believing with a lot of people. That's fine. I was a believer and a knower before anything ever happened to me. I think for anyone who does the right research and looks hard enough and dedicates some time to figuring out the truth, the pieces of the puzzle are going to begin to come together. Some things may not make sense to a few people, but if they keep looking, the pieces will eventually fall in place.

There's a lot about nature that people think they know, but there's a lot more to it than most people realize. I encourage anybody to get out there. Go camping.

Investigate. Take time to be observant. Start looking on the ground.

When they find out what I do, I've had hunters tell me, "I've been in the woods all my life and I've never seen anything like a bigfoot."

The truth is, they aren't looking for sasquatch signs. They're only looking for signs of whatever animal they're hunting. A lot of hunters don't even want to leave their trucks to go to a tree stand. I've had people tell me they've seen bigfoot from their tree stand.

People who don't believe in bigfoot don't look for bigfoot in the woods. They don't look for bigfoot evidence. Then when something happens to them that may be bigfoot related, they can't explain it. They don't give a consideration to the existence of bigfoot. They don't have the possibility in their mind, so the events remain a mystery to them.

When I started doing bigfoot research, I knew I had to go into it with an open mind. When I opened my eyes and senses to see what all is really out there, was when I started finding some evidence. That's when I started finding tracks. It made me want to learn more about sasquatch. I wanted to research more.

In my studies I've learned to compare bears and sasquatches. I believe there are many similarities between their physical characteristics, behavior, diet, feeding habits, and everything else. They are travelers. I've seen a continuous similarity of patterns in where I find bear sign in the woods, I often also find bigfoot sign.

If a person starts to study bears, their activity, and their tracks, they may be surprised to find sasquatch activity in the same area. Here in Virginia, bears are out in full force. Bears are often a source of misidentification when people think they've seen a sasquatch. Their tracks are all over the place. When I start following the bear sign and tracks, I often come upon tracks of sasquatch in the same area.

A lot of people seem to think that I find too much of one thing and it doesn't add up to them. They might look at it from a jealous state of mind. They might even ask themselves, "Why is HE finding all this stuff and other people aren't? He's got to be hoaxing!"

No, I'm not. I've found the pattern that works for me. It has revealed itself to me as a repeating pattern over the years. Follow the bears and their sign, and there will often be squatch activity and signs right there with them. Since this method of exploration works for me, it's something I'm going to stick to.

In one area to which I've been paying a lot of attention and putting this theory to work, I found 16-inch tracks. After I found them, I had to walk all the way back out to get my material to make a cast of the track, then come back into the area.

From an area over to the right of where I was working on casting the tracks, I heard a loud, sharp whistle sound. I stopped and looked over there. Things had been dead quiet, and I found it odd to hear such a loud whistle. I thought to myself, *"It must have been a bird."*

Within 15 feet of the location that contained the tracks, I heard a loud tree knock that stopped me in my tracks. I started looking around at the ground in the area. I thought, *"Wow! The sasquatches are here. They've taken notice of me being here and they are communicating, 'He's back!'"*

I thought about the bird whistle that was so out of place and decided it must have been a squatch. Based on the tracks, the whistle, and the wood knock, I definitely believe there were squatches in that area. I've started paying a lot closer attention in that area.

It was in late November or early December that I found the 16-inch tracks. Then I found some smaller tracks. The next time I returned to the area and camped out around the corner from that locatoin. In one specific area I was looking for more tracks.

Boy, was I blown away! Not only were those 16-inch tracks back, but I measured out 18-inch tracks that were consistent in 3-4 tracks. I measured the stride between footprints and found it to be 68 inches.

I always walk into an area of suspected activity on alert and being very cautious. I did feel as if there was something there watching me in the woods several times in that location.

Daniel Benoit's Personal Sighting

Six friends and I went into that area to do research. We were camping in part of a national forest. We had been to the lake and were coming up the road. I was in front. Shortly after midnight, we had an encounter.

I saw it first and asked myself, *"What the heck was that?"*

I saw the yellow glow in my head lamp but thought about the yellow signs that are posted in some of the trees. Like, "Don't go beyond this point," and so on. For a few seconds I convinced myself that's all it was – those signs reflecting. Then I saw a blink. My heart started pounding.

I said, "Tracy! Ge up here! I've got eye shine." He came and everyone else caught up.

It ran off the roadway we were walking up. We took notice of where it went. It was definitely a juvenile sasquatch about 15 feet from the roadway. We had plenty of light with all our head gear. We were on a rise above the creature. The road sloped down and then leveled off into the woods. We estimated him to be between 4-5 feet tall at the time. Thinking back, he may have been a little taller because we were at an angle looking down toward him.

The behavior was that of a juvenile bouncing around from here to there. There were six of us and we were acting silly trying to get a response from the juvenile sasquatch. He was kind of hyper, swaying back and forth, bouncing around. We continued our silly behavior, hoping to get some kind of interaction with him.

Then I noticed another subject to the far right. We saw him behind the bushes and saw him raise up. We saw eyeshine in the direction where the juvenile had gone. We also saw blinking and could vaguely make out the shape of two others. The eyes were very large and well-spaced apart. The eyes were an amber, yellowish color in the light.

The two bigger ones with him were standing there staring at us and him. We estimated the two larger ones at 6 feet and 8 feet. The largest one also moved his head and turned its head to the left. It looked as if he took a couple of steps before he looked back at us.

It seemed that their behavior toward us was curious. We didn't feel threatened or in harm's way at any time. One couple seemed a little frightened by it all, but the rest of us were fine.

We went back to camp and tried to debunk the whole thing. We discussed every known animal in that area and none of them fit.

We did come back the next day in the daylight to try to get a height comparison. We did our best but realize that some of our estimates may have been off. Estimating at night and then trying to do the comparisons in the day leaves a little room for inaccuracy.

We were all convinced that what we saw was a small family unit of squatches.

Squatch activity seems to be picking up.

I've gotten reports from other people who don't even know me or my experiences there who tell me about encounters they've had in the same general location. Some of the reports are older and some are more recent.

Many have found structures or formations in the forest appearing to be possible shelters. All are equal to behaviors and socializations of the known primates. Since bigfoot is not acknowledged by scientists today, there is no classification of what sasquatch or bigfoot is. There is no specific identification.

I do not consider our big hairy forest dwelling subject to be one of the known primates. However, I do compare the two, and in doing so believe undoubtedly that bigfoot is a form of ape, but an independent species. Sasquatches are not human by any means.

In my research, I have discovered many details that correlate with known facts about primates. However, all of it is still considered speculation due to the lack of scientific involvement in the field. It is for this very reason the ECBRO has set in motion the *Discovery Project* and has gathered a sincere, honest, and dedicated team.

Prior to introducing myself as a researcher in the bigfoot world, I was no more than a solo field researcher who grew up spending most of my time in nature. I explored, hiked, and hunted.

When I went on to establish an organization in 2011, it was dedicated to research and seeking truth about the subject of bigfoot and the unknown world surrounding this existence. We believe in the truth that an unknown elusive primate surely does roam our woodlands and our own back yards. Evidence has been gathered and analyzed, as well as other un-natural finds.

Even in accepting a margin of error, we believe the sightings reported to us are at least 90% true and accurate based on studies and observations in the field.

Perhaps this taste of information and conviction of the reality of bigfoot will enlighten the reader to the true dedication we have in the field of Cryptozoology. The ECBRO are not experts in this field but are always researching and studying to bring the truth to light. We seek public support as well as patience as we continue in our mission to provide logical, clear, and real evidence. This has always been our effort to do so. We believe in educating and bringing awareness to both the bigfoot community and to the close minded in the world around us.

Primarily we focus our studies and research of this subject on the east coast of the United States. We also promote many other outside groups for the purpose of studying our elusive subject. The ECBRO has grown to include research teams outside the United States who we proudly acknowledge as they share their research and findings with the rest of the team. The ECBRO team has become global and will work together for the expansion of research throughout the world.

We welcome any and all who choose or request membership and are willing to share the truth with us all.

Favorite quotes from Daniel Benoit:

"If you don't know what is known, then how can you seek what is considered to be unknown."

Another quote he lives by and shares often was said by Les Stroud: "Don't fall prey to deception."

Good Ones and Bad Ones
Dana J. Southern

I didn't see the creature or hear it, but my children told me the story about a bigfoot incident that happened to them on some of our family's property. I believe them. I may not have seen one personally, but I know they're here.

My husband, Tony, trained me. He said to always remember that a bear stinks like an outhouse, but a booger is worse. There's a lot of other creatures in the woods than people realize.

I've been born and raised to know there are more than "lions, and tigers, and bears… Oh, my!"

I wish I could remember every story anyone has ever told me, especially when my daughter worked in the Bigfoot Museum.

I met a man with a rich Native American heritage and blood line who was trained to know the difference between the good bigfoot and the bad ones. He said a person can tell if the bigfoot is a good one by its dark or golden eyes. A bad one has red eyes.

Some of them are guardians.

He said that there are certain people who have the ability to know creatures and creatures know that person.

He is a big, big man. He lives way out from me and has a lot of farmland. He wouldn't be scared of anything. He's about 6'6" and a big old dude.

He told me a bigfoot came into his yard, picked up a huge hog, and took it with him. This man followed him. He said it was going through the woods, crashing through the trees, carrying this big old hog.

He said, "I walked up on this ravine while I was following the bigfoot, and suddenly it was gone! That's when I realized there must be places or portals these creatures pass through. He was huge, and the hog he was carrying was huge. How else could they both have disappeared?"

"I've seen big ones and little ones, red ones, black ones, and brownish looking ones. My aunt told me that a person must see them with their heart and not with their eyes. If I close my eyes, I can talk to them. I know what they're saying."

It sounds like telepathy. They communicate without speaking.

He said he asked one, "What do you need?"

The bigfoot answered, "We're just watching."

This same man was at a funeral last year and had a young boy with him. He looked at me and cut his eyes sideways at me like, "Will you tell her…?"

The boy shook his head in a definite, "No way!" He had seen one while he was staying at this man's house. He saw them talking.

These things are out there - the woolyboogers, the things in the shadows that make you think, *"Did I just see what I think I saw?"*

This man's aunt has died. I wish I could have talked to her about these things. She knew a lot about them. She knew many stories. The Native Americans always had stories about these creatures.

To the indigenous people, these creatures are part of their legends across generations. I often tell people that where there is a legend, there is a greater truth. It's left up to us to figure out that truth and where or how the legend got started.

In the Bible it talks about "everything that creepeth" – everything in the ocean; everything on the land… We don't really know what that means. Who's to say that these creatures weren't among what God created?

When you read in the Bible about the sons of God coming into the daughters of man, there are a lot of questions. That's why bestiality was so bad. Imagine what could result from different species interbreeding.

Public Domain Image of a Road Sign

My Camera Refused to Display
what My Eyes Were Looking At
Brian Long

I saw my first individual in Brooksville, Florida.

To make a very detailed story fit here, I was researching tree structures.

The one I was stuck on could have been caused by events in nature, pictured in the story. I was stressing over trying to figure it out in February. I had been on site for a while and it was pushing 4:00 p.m. I decided to give up and say nature formed the structure.

I stopped studying it and just took a step back to look at nature's beauty around me. I looked up and dead in front of me were two sasquatches facing me 40 yards away.

I started shaking. They never moved a muscle. I pulled my cell/camera up and tried to get a picture. Nothing was there in the picture!

"WHAT??? How can this be?" I asked myself.

I pulled the camera down looking with my naked eye and there they were! I played this unbelievable game four more times.

I wanted a clear picture!

I walked quickly to my truck grabbed the binoculars and went back to where I was standing a few moments earlier. Mind you my truck was not 100 feet away. I pulled my binoculars up and the image on the right was a palmetto bush with foliage missing in the shape of head and shoulders.

I put the binoculars on the left-hand image, and nothing was there either! I thought to myself, *"My first sighting and I blew it!"*

I was really upset with myself for not getting video. Ok, I was really disappointed but common sense kicked in hard. This was a Friday and the night before I watched a Todd Standing video about sasquatches killing humans!

I ran to my truck shaking because if he or she wasn't in front of me where the heck was he or she? I couldn't see them, but that didn't mean they couldn't see me!

This tree looks simple just leaning against another tree. I have no idea how far a sasquatch shoved that tree into the sand, but I couldn't budge it. And I am a big boy.

The office worker at the Withlacoochie Ranger station can verify two things. I visited her twice. She told me about a sighting two nights before I showed up there.

The gentleman who had the sighting said to her, "SOMETHING CROSSED THE ROAD IN MY HEADLIGHTS VERY TALL, DARK, AND HAIRY. I won't say what it was, but it crossed Route 41 in 2 steps!"

I want to say to the public, these sasquatch people are everywhere. I saw my first tree structure alongside Interstate 90 between Cleveland, Ohio, and Erie, Pennsylvania. That tree structure was the most notable one I've seen including on the Internet. It was an X with the handle end of a trident stuck between the bottom of the X.

Tridents don't just appear on their own. I believe I've seen four in three years on the internet. These structures are something special.

My wife and I are full-time recreational vehicle travelers which is why we've been all over and had these experiences in different places.

My First Bigfoot Encounter
Matthew Delph
(Mountain Empire Cryptid Research Organization)
(M.E.C.R.O.)

I was born and raised in Indiana about an hour south of Chicago. I didn't believe in anything about bigfoot. If there was such a creature, I thought it might be alive and live out in the Himalayan Mountains. I just thought bigfoot was based on folklore and stuff like that. I thought that whatever and wherever it was, it certainly wasn't living in Indiana.

My siblings and I grew up on a dead-end gravel road. Our house was the very last house on the road. Our nearest neighbor was fields away from us. We were surrounded all around our house by nothing but woods. A doctor owned hundreds of acres around our place, and he never let anyone hunt on his land.

I grew up hunting and fishing. My dad used to do some trapping for a while. I was very familiar with wildlife and being in the outdoors.

Sugar Creek ran right behind our house. It ran into the Wabash River. Right where the Wabash River and the Tippecanoe River met was called River Junction. The creek behind our house, Sugar Creek, ran straight into them.

The terrain was flat, but around the creek it was low. There was a kind of plateau. Cedar trees grew there, brush that was really thick, and other plants. There was a field of raspberry bushes that had a lot of thorns.

We had nothing but woods around us. We had some cornfields nearby, an old apple orchard back in there, some old houses and building structures. We had hogs, chickens, and that kind of livestock on our place.

We didn't notice anything odd around the house until the late 1980s or early 1990s. We had been flooded out a couple of times. We started hearing weird screams, the dogs barking at nothing we knew of.

We never imagined the unusual things happening were coming from a bigfoot. In our minds, such a creature wasn't real. In our thoughts, bigfoot would have been the same as vampires, werewolves, or any other mythical kind of thing.

There was a field that we always cut down, plowed, and put a garden in. We were allowed to play around our house, in the fields, and around the garden area. But we were not supposed to go beyond that.

There was one time when my little brother, little sister, and the neighbor kid were out playing and went further than they were supposed to. They got on the doctor's land. They were playing in the woods and thought they heard something. They got back in late.

My little sister, brother, and the neighbor kid all said, "A monster chased us out of the woods!"

Of course, my parents thought they were just saying that because they had been where they weren't supposed to be and thought they were going to get in trouble. Our parents thought an animal like a deer, or something had spooked them.

The way they told it was that they heard a noise in the bushes but couldn't see what was causing it. Then it started shaking the bushes and throwing rocks at them. When it started screaming, they got a glimpse of something big and dark, but they couldn't really tell what it was. It scared them so bad, they took off. It ran them out of the woods.

We didn't think much about it. They were just kids who got out where they shouldn't have been, got in trouble, and that was the end of it.

One night we were sitting in the house and the dogs started barking and going off. We didn't have air conditioning in the house at that time. We had box fans in the windows to try to cool things down. For those not familiar with these, the window had to be open and the fan was inserted in the opening. We heard screaming coming through the window fan from the woods.

We didn't know what it was, but for sure no one thought it was a bigfoot. I wish I had known back then what I know now.

We used to go play in the fields and the woods freely. We found four or five "grass beds" that looked as if something had flattened the grass out where it had been laying. These spots were huge. As kids, we thought it was a spot where a bunch of deer had been lying down for the night. The strangest thing about those spots was the odor that was in them.

As I got older into my teenage years, I did a lot of deer hunting. I started coming across a lot of weird stuff.

I got after one deer that was a 21-pointer! It was a huge deer. I never got him, but I did get his antler sheds. So, when I was out there hunting I was always looking for this elusive buck.

Sometimes I would smell this awful smell when I was out in the woods. There was nothing else like it that I had ever smelled to identify it. I had no idea what animal the stench was coming from.

I also remember finding long hairs caught up high in the barbed wire fences. It wasn't fur. It was like hair on top of the barbed wire. A coyote, or any other animal that I knew of always crawled under a barbed wire fence. I couldn't imagine what was getting hairs caught up that high on the fence.

As the years went on, we'd find dead deer. Nobody was allowed to hunt out there, but we'd find deer something (animal) had killed. Our dogs would drag in deer with broken backs. Strange things such as that happened.

I think the dogs kept whatever strange creatures that were out there away from the immediate area around the house. When I started to go deer hunting, I'd put the dogs up. If I didn't, they'd follow me and scare the deer away.

I had a favorite trail I liked to hunt. Some truly unexplainable things happened while I was out hunting. I'd hear unidentified screams. I'd smell these nasty smells.

But I still didn't know what any of those things meant or how to connect the dots to find the answer.

After I graduated from high school I moved to Colorado. My parents moved down south. After a few months, I moved back to Indiana although my parents had moved away. I was staying with my friend, Chris.

I always went back to the old home place to deer hunt with my friends. The unknown creature was still out there, but we were so used to the odd things that happened, we really didn't give them much thought.

The week-end before Thanksgiving in 1996, on a Saturday afternoon, my life changed forever. I never knew what was out there until I saw it with my own eyes.

My buddy, Chris, couldn't go hunting with me that day. He had his daughter with him. He wanted to spend time with her.

I was 21 and not afraid to go deer hunting alone. It was a beautiful, sunny day on the week-end before Thanksgiving. If I wanted to deer hunt in Indiana, I had to go then because I would be going the following week to have Thanksgiving with my family in Virginia.

I came to a tree that I always liked to lean against when I was hunting. It was so thick up in there that I couldn't use a tree stand or anything like that. The tree was my spot. I got there about 2:30 in the afternoon.

I had my plan for a successful hunt. I had scouted out the area so well that I knew there were deer that would pass through the area every two to three days and right there was where I could get a shot. I deliberately planned my hunting endeavors around the days that I knew the deer would cycle through.

That afternoon, according to my scouting, there should have been deer in the area. There was nothing. Everything was dead. Nothing moving. Quiet. No animal activity. Nothing at all.

That went on all afternoon. It started getting dusk and I decided since I hadn't seen a thing all day long it was time to pack up my stuff and go home. I thought I must have miscalculated the day they'd be passing through, or maybe the deer had smelled me. Something was definitely wrong.

As I was gathering my stuff and getting ready to leave, this nasty odor came through the air again. I had smelled it before, but I never knew what it was. It smelled like rotting hay, something really musty or mildewed. Nasty.

It really didn't trigger any kind of fear in me because I had smelled it before. I just thought, *"There's that odor again."*

I heard a couple of sticks break close to where I was sitting, I was really close to the trail. On the other side of the trail was a bunch of cedar trees and small saplings mixed in. It was so thick in that spot that deer would have to come right up on you before you would see them.

I heard sticks and stuff breaking so I thought, *"There's a doe coming through here. She's going to pass this way."*

I got my gun up ready to fire off a shot and hoping I would see something. The tree breaking got louder. The bushes were shaking. Whatever it was, it was getting more aggressive.

I was trying to figure it out. *"There must be a buck in there following the doe!"*

I kept looking, sitting there patiently waiting for the big buck to waltz out in front of me. Whatever it was, its behavior got more aggressive the closer it came. Trees were shaking. Tree branches were snapping. Saplings were snapping.

My thought was, *"It must be two bucks fighting over this doe!"*

I was so excited! I thought maybe it was the big buck I had seen before. Or if there were two bucks fighting, maybe I would get to see them both and shoot the bigger one.

The disturbance quit. Then I heard a sound like a cross between a high-pitched scream and a deep growl. It was a sound that cut right through me! I had heard screams before, but none of them was aggressive like this one was.

I was thinking, *"What in the world is this?"*

I heard stuff falling behind me, but when I looked back, I couldn't see anything. I did see trees being shaken and could hear the sound of trees snapping.

Less than thirty yards away from me there was a gap in between two cedar trees. Whatever it was coming toward me was headed that way and stepped into the gap. I saw the creature and estimated it to have been between 6-7 feet tall.

The sun was setting. The evening sun was hitting this thing in the back. I could see its form, but its face was more shadow like. I could see long dark hair. It reminded me of a tall, lanky orangutang. It had a rounded head – not the cone shaped one that some people use to describe a bigfoot. I could see the long hair hanging off its head and onto its shoulders. It had two arms, but I couldn't see the legs because of the tall grass that was in there.

When it moved, it glided like a small plastic store bag caught up in the wind in a parking lot. That's how the thing moved across the 15-foot gap. It glided across, very smoothly.

As soon as it got to the edge it was partially covered up again, but I could still see the shoulder, the arm, and the long hair. It let out another screaming deep growl. I still had my gun up. I was looking at it and still very confused. I was scared, but more confused.

I was thinking, *"WHAT IS THAT???"*

It threw a stick at me that was about three feet long and had a diameter like a baseball bat. It went flying by my head super-fast. It would have done some damage if it would have hit me.

Then it screamed again.

I thought, *"I don't know what it is, but it does NOT want me here!"*

So, I took off running down the trail. I got to the point where I had to cross the creek and I turned around to see if I was going to have to shoot or have to fight. I had to know if it was still after me.

I didn't see it anywhere, but as soon as I stopped it let out another scream with that growl in it. I knew that it was still, there, still watching me. So, I took off out of there.

I got back to my friend Chris's house and sat down.

He took one look at me and said, "What's wrong with you?"

I said, "What do you mean?"

He said, "I can tell something is wrong with you."

I told him, "I don't know how to explain it, but I've seen something."

He said, "What did you see?"

I said, "You are probably not going to believe me if I tell you!"

Chris said, "Dude! I've hunted out there with you. What was it?"

I said, "I don't know! It was like a monster! It was a big hairy thing like a monster."

That's the only way I knew how to describe it. That's the day that changed my life forever. That's when I started researching to find answers about what I had seen. That's when I started down this big rabbit hole I'm in now.

Mountain Empire Cryptid Research Organization (MECRO) came out of that experience eventually.

I don't believe there are that many of these creatures out there, like some people say. I don't get involved with a lot of other bigfoot groups because some of them think they see one every day they go out in the woods!

I have learned a lot about bigfoot in my years since that one incident. They travel the waterways. There's usually a small group of them together – three, four, or five. Over the years I have been able to put some of the pieces together. They move around a lot.

Finding a bigfoot is kind of like trying to find a needle in a haystack that keeps moving.

Through the wintertime in Indiana, I used to rabbit hunt. Usually after the first of December until March or April, there is no activity in the area where my encounter took place. I've gone back to investigate based on what happened to me and where. These creatures move out of the area during that time. We would hear no screams, smell no funky smells, and find no footprints during that time of the year.

When we would start mushroom hunting or planting a garden in the springtime, all through the summer and into the fall we would hear the screams and smell that awful smell from time to time. During hunting season was when there would be the most activity. These things had gone on all the time before I had my encounter, but until then we never knew what it was.

There was no activity in the wintertime.

I've seen stuff through thermal imaging devices. I've had rocks thrown at me. I've had to develop a different approach to go looking for these things. I try to go with recent sightings. Sometimes I get a tip from a local veterinary clinic that lets me know when they've had a report of livestock kills and certain things like that.

The odds of seeing a bigfoot are very rare. They are out there, but not nearly as many as people tend to think. There are a lot of different species of different creatures out there that I've learned through the years. Bigfoot is just one of many.

They're Real
Ed Brown (YouTube Talk Show Host)

If a person happened to go out into the woods looking for bigfoot and heard a large animal walking in the woods, they cannot attribute those sounds alone to bigfoot. However, if they hear a large animal walking in the woods, branches deliberately being broken, and vocalizations, the sum total of those things would most likely come from a true bigfoot encounter. Cumulatively, all these things together scream bigfoot. Individually, none of those things are proof without an actual sighting.

On a ten-day excursion in Oregon, a lot of cool things happened to us. A buddy of mine, Dan Lindholm, and I had gone up to the base of Mount Magoplin. It's a very nice place. There is a nice campground there right on the lake. Most people who go stay right there.

There are parts of the lake where probably no one has ever been. That's the area that we were drawn to.

Dan took his boat out there one day and we took it to a part of the lake that looked like no one had been there in decades. There was mossy ground and absolutely no trails of any kind. We went back in there and we did hear some movement, but there was nothing definitive. It was such a beautiful spot. It just goes to prove that as the crow flies, about two miles from the publicly preferred campground was this beautiful, untouched part of the wilderness. There are remote spots such as this across the country where bigfoot would be at home and for the most part undisturbed.

We had gone to the camping site we use there which is nowhere near the official campsite that everyone else uses. In advance of our trip we had set out about 13-15 trail cameras and left them out for about 90 days. Then we went back and gathered all of them but one. We don't know what happened to the missing one.

On the trail cams we got images of a big, beautiful, cinnamon colored bear. It came right up to the camera and sniffed it. We got pictures of big bucks walking by. We even got a picture of a mountain lion, which I didn't even know were in that area. There were beautiful birds in the images as well. The kinds of animals that make their homes there in the wilderness are phenomenal.

On one of the cameras we did get an interesting anomaly. There were two trees that were about three feet apart. We had set two trail cameras up, one on each tree facing the same direction, then tipped them out about 10-15° to get a larger area in view, but still be able to put the images together for a whole picture.

At one point when we were watching what was on the cameras, Dan's camera started getting a lot of static. All we could see was static.

That camera got fried. We were never able to use it again or figure out what had happened to it. My camera, the one on the left, picked up movement on the right side of the camera, but it's very quick and we just couldn't make out what it was.

That's another point about bigfoot. If you get something on camera and you think it's bigfoot, but you can't see it well enough to be positive that it's bigfoot, then you certainly shouldn't claim that it is. Still, that was quite interesting.

One night while we were out there we were sitting by the fire. Dan had his guitar out and was playing it. Out in the distance to our north, we heard a really loud guttural screaming, as if someone was really angry. After about ten seconds it quit. Then at about the same distance of probably a mile away and 15° difference, there came a response.

Our location and the location of the first scream and the position of the second scream seemed to form a triangle with us at the lower tip. They went back and forth for about ten minutes.

We were like, "Holy cow!"

We got our recorders out and were so excited because we knew we were going to get those vocalizations on audio and be able to get it all analyzed. After it was over, of course, there was nothing on the audio. This absolutely blows my mind because it was very loud. Why the recorders didn't pick it up, I have no idea.

Dan keeps very good notes on our trips. He is dedicated to the importance of documenting everything. He noted the time, date, etc. That was a very interesting experience. If we could hear the loud screams so clearly with our human ears, why didn't our professional equipment pick it up?

On another trip in the exact same spot, we were camping out and heard some noises coming from the other side of the trail from where we were camping. It was deep in the woods.

There was another guy with us that time. I asked him if he would hold the camera, the fleer, and keep it on me so that he could see me going into that area across from our campsite. I wanted to see if I could get anything to move and he could catch it on fleer.

He says, "Alright. I can do that." So, he starts telling me, "Go right… go left…" and was telling me where to go over the walkie talkie.

I had no flashlight, no gun, no weapon of any kind. All I had with me was a walkie talkie and was completely in the dark. So, I kept walking and there was a clearing about 40-50 yards away from where we were camping.

As soon as I stepped into that clearing, something whistled at me. I kind of stepped back. It was in the middle of the night. Pitch black. Birds don't whistle under those circumstances. They don't go out chirping at night.

I thought, *"What in the world is that?"*

I stepped into the clearing again, and the whistle came again. I stepped back. We repeated the sequence about three or four times.

I got on the radio and said, "Guys! Something weird is going on. Every time I step into this clearing area something is whistling at me! I'm going to do it again and if it whistles at me this time, I'm just going to keep going."

There was no whistle until I stepped into the area. That was very odd. I walked right on out into the clearing and it didn't whistle again after I got into the clearing. So, I was standing there and heard a little bit of noise.

I said over the walkie talkie, "Guys, are you picking up anything on the fleer?"

They said, "No."

All of a sudden on my left, in the same direction that we'd heard the screaming coming from the other night, something came running through the woods toward me.

We call this behavior a bluff charge which bigfoot have been known to do when they want to scare someone out of an area. It sounded like an elk coming through the trees breaking branches with its horns. It was unnaturally loud and seemed extremely aggressive.

I didn't know what to do except to turn toward it and prepare to fight whatever was coming at me if I could. There was no way I could outrun it in the dark. Then it just stopped. I never saw anything. I never heard anything else. It didn't make a noise like a grunt or anything like that.

All I know is that SOMETHING came charging through those woods very hard and very fast. Then it just stopped right beyond my sight. I'd have to say that was the scariest thing I've ever experienced there.

Another night we had set up some recorders around the campsite. We had the whole thing planned precisely.

We had about ten of the recorders in a circle around the perimeter of our campsite. So, if anything happened, we'd at least get the audio of something coming at us. If something yelled off in the distance, we should pick it up on audio. That was our plan.

There was a small weather station about 50-75 yards from where we were camping that night. It had different types of metal poles around it like a fence pole, a flagpole, and other types of poles they apparently use in detecting the weather. On the recording we started picking up this *"ping... ping... ping..."*

We thought, "What in the world is that?"

So, we went over there to investigate, and saw some metal poles. We thought, *"There had to be something hitting those poles."*

Maybe something was hitting them with rocks. So, I tried to imitate the sound. I picked up some rocks and threw at the poles. No, that wasn't what the recording sounded like. Then I finally hit one pole with a very thin rock. That was the only one which duplicated the sound and we had heard it repeatedly.

In the wilds of Oregon, there is no creature with the exception of human beings that has the dexterity to hold something with its thumbs and tap on metal. It couldn't have been a raccoon. They are hyper and rapid. This type of animal would have produced a flurry of sounds together instead of evenly spaced out tapping.

We never figured out what it was, but something had to be hitting that pole with a flat rock. A thick rock or a round rock did not produce the same sound.

All of the previous things I've mentioned happened in that same area where we like to camp near the base of Mount Magoplin.

Southern Oregon is extremely active with bigfoot sightings, encounters, and stories. I've been to several places and have had weird experiences in every single one, including seeing something that I can't say for sure what it was. I can't say it was a bigfoot and I can't say it wasn't.

It wasn't dark yet, but it was late. I saw something move from one tree to another. Could it have been a bear? I don't know. I'm very careful not to falsely claim a bigfoot sighting if I am not absolutely sure of what I saw.

In this area there is a lake. We go hiking there at times. The hike goes around the lake and is about 10 miles and forms a big circle.

One day when we were hiking, we found three separate tracks. All of them were exactly the same in length – about 15 inches long and 7 ½ inches wide at the ball of the foot. They all had toe impressions as well as heel and forefoot. The ground is very hard out there and it's difficult to find any prints at all from any of the animals that live there.

It was amazing that in one day we found three. Two were from a right foot and one was from a left foot. We found them about a mile and a half apart from each other. It was as if something had walked right around through there on the path we happened to be on that circled around the lake and we just happened to be walking around the trail and found three of the prints.

That was pretty cool. It was an unusual find for that area.

Again, I want to stress that if a person sees one peculiar thing, hears one noise, or gets a glimpse of something quickly that they're not sure of, they can't just assume or say, "That's bigfoot!"

Good footprints are a very important find. They are the kind of evidence that speaks for itself.

If a lot of different things happen at the same time and in the same place, cumulatively, add them all together and it probably does equal a bigfoot. When all of the pieces match, there's only one thing it could be.

We went out there one day during our ten-day trip and another guy had come to join us for a couple of days while we were there. With the three of us out doing field research, we were kind of in a triangular formation probably about 15 yards apart from each other while we were in the field. We were able to look for more signs of bigfoot that way than all bunched up together.

Dan said, "Something just threw a rock at me." It had landed pretty close to him.

I said, "Seriously?"

He said, "Yeah. Turn your camera on."

I turned it on (I do have this on video) and another good-sized rock whizzed past me and landed close by. I ran over to check it out. In a space of about ten minutes, we had five rocks thrown at us.

I didn't know anything about that part of the area where we were at in that moment. I said, "I hear something running through water. It sounds like somebody in water up to their knees!"

Dan said, "There's no water up there. There's no pond and no lake."

We walked in the direction that I'd distinctly heard the sound to investigate. I was the only one who had heard it, but I was sure of the sound of someone running through water.

We walked up there and sure enough, there was a drainage line running through the place which was about six feet deep and had about four feet of water in it! That thing which had been throwing rocks at us could have jumped into that drain "creek" and then ran down the creek out of our eyesight. There was no way anyone could have seen it running down through there unless they had been up beside of it and looking at the drain.

I felt like something had deliberately jumped into that water and ran down through it, because that's exactly what I heard. Altogether, it adds up to possibly be a genuine bigfoot encounter. Sill, without actually seeing the creature, we can't be 100% certain.

Someone asked if I was ever afraid when we're out like that. I'd be lying if I said it wasn't a little scary at times.

I'm a skeptical believer. I know bigfoot is real. I know they're out there. But I'm not willing to chalk up every oddity or unexplained thing that happens in the woods as a bigfoot encounter. As I shared in the first *Bigfoot and Woolybooger Tales* book, I saw my first bigfoot in Harlan County Kentucky. I KNOW they're real. BUT – I'm always very careful NOT to say something was a bigfoot encounter or experience unless I see the creature and know for sure that's what it is.

Even though I have been scared on occasion, like the night I went into that open clearing area by myself, I'm the kind of person who is compelled to go check things out. I had no flashlight, no weapon, and nothing to defend myself. Had it been a bear charging at me and had come out of the woods, I was toast. There's nothing I could have done to protect myself. I'd be gone. Did that scare me? Yes, indeed it did!

We never take a weapon like a firearm with us when we go out. I've carried a knife from time to time, but it's more for the camping experience than it is for a weapon. It has a little saw edge on one side for sawing branches for firewood. I've never really thought of it as a weapon.

There are a lot of people who do go into the woods armed when they're in search of bigfoot because they are scared, or because they think they're going to be the one to capture or kill a bigfoot. They fantasize about making a million dollars off of it by becoming famous.

If anybody is willing to take the time and do a little research, they will find that in almost every state it would be illegal to kill this creature. The law in most states doesn't mention bigfoot, but it does say what the animals are that a person CAN hunt. If an animal is not on that list, the only way a person could kill it and not get in big trouble is if the creature were attacking them… self-defense.

If people are looking for bigfoot and see one walking in the trees and then take a shot at it, that is NOT self-defense. That person will go to jail.

There are a lot of crazy stories out there about people with aggressive or irrational behavior.

One story I've heard is about three people who went bigfoot hunting and took guns with them. One of the guys was coming out of the woods and another one of them saw him and thought he was bigfoot. He shot and killed his friend!

I've heard there was a guy who dressed up like bigfoot to put on a hoax in Montana and he got hit by a car and died. He was wearing a ghillie suit, trying to make somebody think he was a bigfoot and died because of it.

If somebody is going to get involved in bigfoot field research, then they need to take it seriously. They should never go out thinking like G.I. Joe and acting like they're going to go find a bigfoot, kill it, get famous, and get rich because of it. The truth is, if they should do it, they are most likely to end up in jail.

The chances of hunting for a bigfoot and finding one, then getting a shot at it are likely impossible. They are too smart, too well camouflaged, too sneaky, too elusive, and too fast.

Derek Randles runs the Olympic Project in Washington State. Their purpose in this organization is to "document the existence of Sasquatch through science and investigation." They do habitat studies, collect DNA samples, and set out a lot of game cameras. They also do public education. I've been told that Derek conducted an experiment which shows how hard it is to get a good photo or film of a bigfoot. There were 8-9 people with him who were going to go on a hike.

A real bigfoot usually knows people are there long before they know he is there. These creatures are very elusive. Most sightings lats only a few seconds.

Derek told them up front to "Get your cameras ready. There's someone in the woods right now in a bigfoot suit. At some point, he's going to run out in front of us. Let's see who can get the best picture of him."

He had told them what was going to happen. They knew to expect the guy in the bigfoot suit to pop out at some time during the hike. They knew to have their cameras ready. Out of the whole group, one person got a picture of a blurred figure as it went behind a tree.

In the bigfoot research world, there are deliberate hoaxers. There have been those who put a lot of time and energy in the effort to convince people that false information is true. Some individuals seem to find their falsified information and public response to it entertaining.

One guy claimed he had killed a bigfoot baby that turned out to be a bear. He had to know it was a bear. There are fake reports out there, sensationalized claims about things that didn't really happen. There are fake videos, and photos of people dressed to look like bigfoot.

It makes people not want to take seriously what authentic and sincere researchers are doing. If we can't take it seriously, why should the public?

It appears that scientists and governmental departments in the field of big game and wildlife do not believe in anything bigfoot related. One of the theories I've heard, perhaps the most notable, is that if they discover a new species of something that's not supposed to exist, it could impact the lumber industry, natural gas pipeline projects, and so on. Those industries would be seriously impacted because that rare species would have to be protected.

The spotted owl that was discovered in Washington and part of Canada brought a screeching halt to the lumber industry in that area. They are still feeling the impact of it. It not only upended the lumber industry but took away jobs and impacted the economy.

Another plausible reason I've heard would be that if the government admitted that there are bigfoot or black panthers roaming around in the wild, people would start thinking, "There are dangerous creatures out there! I'm not going out!"

People could potentially avoid national parks, campgrounds, wilderness activities of many kinds, and the economy would be negatively impacted through the breach in the tourism industry. Or on the opposite end, these family-oriented places might be overwhelmed with "crazies" trying to locate and kill one.

If nobody proves or admits that these unexplained species exist, then they don't have to deal with it. When no one was talking about bigfoot or sasquatch in a modern-day context, there wasn't a problem. It could all be written off as legend or mythology. The interest in bigfoot research has grown exponentially since the 1970s. It is getting harder to ignore so many eyewitness accounts.

The official denial may be a result of everything combined. I have no explanation for why there continues to be denial of the existence of bigfoot. The reasons I just mentioned are only theories I've heard on the question.

Sometimes hunters will say to me, "I've been a hunter all my life and been in the woods all my life. I don't believe in bigfoot because I've never seen one in all these years. Bigfoot is not real."

I say, "How do you know? You might have been in the woods and heard something walking 20 yards away that you heard and did not see. What you thought was a bear might have been a bigfoot. You might have heard sticks breaking or smelled a horrible smell that you didn't recognize and ignored it because you didn't know what it was. All of these things could potentially be bigfoot activity, but because you're so closed off to it, you don't even consider the possibility or probability that bigfoot might be linked to these things."

I think it's irresponsible for someone to make a claim based on being uninformed or misinformed on the topic. If someone wants to talk to me or even debate with me about whether bigfoot is real or not, they'd better do a little research first. If they don't, I'll bury them in the debate.

If a person is uninformed about something because they haven't done the research or tried to discover the truth for themselves, or even allowed themselves to be in a place where they may have their own experiences, then they have no right to tell someone who claims to have seen one, "I haven't seen a bigfoot, so bigfoot is not real. You didn't see one. You're mistaken."

Accusing people of misidentification is also very frustrating. Big dark hairy things walking on two legs with the ability to communicate with each other is hard to misidentify or confuse with a bear, a coyote, or a dog.

The worst critics are usually people who have no experience or informed thoughts on the subject to back them up. All they have is their own biased opinion based on what they have not experienced personally or based on what someone else has said to them.

There are too many things that happen to people in the woods that have no other logical explanation than their word of what happened and what they've seen with their own eyes. I could take a skeptic to the places in Oregon where there has been so much activity, or to Alabama where I was with a group of five that had an experience, and I'm pretty sure they'd change their mind.

Bigfoot is real.

Public domain images

Public Domain Image

Return to Nature to Sooth My Grief
Jimmy Blanton
(Unknown and Cryptid Research Society
of Southeastern Kentucky)

My beloved wife and grade school sweetheart, Melissa, passed away in September 2019 and I needed to get back to nature to clear my head. I was still grieving at that time and had my train of thought on her.

I was told by several of my cryptid research friends that if you keep looking for the creature we call bigfoot you will run into him or her one day. I got the shock of my life on a cold January day in 2020.

I have been an active bigfoot field researcher for six years. I have heard and seen many crazy things in my lifetime - things I can't explain. I witnessed something that I thought I would never see.

I walked to an area that I had been to many times. There was a small hilltop from which I could look over from time to time and watch the area deer and black bear at a distance.

I was quiet, trying not to disturb anything in the area. I noticed it was quiet - crazy quiet - but didn't think anything deeply about it because my mind was elsewhere.

I thought I would stay in that spot for a while. I set down my walking stick and backpack. I got my tripod and cell phone out to make a video. I noticed something over the hill. It was a reddish-brown and appeared to be a bear looking at the ground. I noticed also that it was doing something on the ground in front of it.

When I stood up to step behind a log and observe the bear, the animal stood up. It was 7 feet tall! All kinds of thoughts ran through my mind.

"What is this? Is that a bigfoot?" My eyes and my brain were struggling to get in the same place.

I suppose those thoughts were the normal things a person's mind would try to process and to make sense of in that kind of unexpected situation. Then it dawned on me that the creature I was looking at had legs and arms. They were much smaller than the torso, but the shoulders were very broad.

I didn't notice a smell, which is one classic sign people often speak of experiencing in advance of a sighting of this elusive creature. It finally sunk into my mind, *"Bigfoot! Holy cow! It IS a bigfoot!"*

With that excitement I moved my foot without meaning to and made a sound. The creature turned its head slightly to the left but not enough for me to see any facial features. In the shock I was in I had made my mind up to grab my stuff and back up and get out of there! Forget trying to get photos or pictures! I wanted to put some distance between me and the creature I was looking at.

I had just placed my right hand on my walking stick and my left hand on my backpack when it heard me. The creature's response was to run. This thing ran so fast it was out of sight in five seconds. It amazed me at how quickly it could move and be gone from sight.

It has taken me months to get up the courage to go back to my research area. This time examining the area where bigfoot had stood, I noticed a rock and cracked empty acorn shells. Could the creature use a rock in that manner? They are said to be stealthy creatures that show an intelligence that is shocking.

I will return to that area one day for a third time. For now, I play that day like a broken record in my mind.

I was asked by a friend if I did get any video that day, but that was the furthest from my mind at that time. My video equipment was still in the backpack. After the whole thing was over, I did remember I had my cell phone in my front pants pocket the whole time!

This incident showed me the actual mindset of the bigfoot witness. Those who have seen the creature have told me the same has happened to them. In that situation a phone can be in the front or back pocket, or in your hand, but you don't think about it when you see something that you are told at a young age doesn't exist.

Editor's Note:

Jimmy Blanton is the founder of Unknown and Cryptid Research Society of Southeastern Kentucky from Harlan, Kentucky. He is the Crypto Con founder and owner. He is also podcast host of Wildlife Enthusiasts, Fisherman, and Outdoorsman.

Statue of the Woodbooger at High Knob – Norton, Virginia
Photo by Judith Victoria Hensley

Booger Chronicles
Our Life Among the Sasquatches
Kelly C.
*(requested to remain anonymous to protect the location of
the property and sightings listed in this story)*

We have sasquatch on our property. I am choosing
not to disclose my full name or my exact location because
I don't want people coming to harass or hurt them.

I don't want to sound like some weird person about
any of this. I've spent twenty years in the healthcare
profession, have a PhD and am a logical, level-headed
person.

But then, I saw a sasquatch. I call them boogers. I
grew up with the term "boogers," referring to the same
creatures. We've had a lot of booger related incidents on
our property.

My husband has lived on this property all his life.
He's always heard tree knocks and things that he didn't

think that much about. The woods make noise. He took it all in as part of the sounds of nature.

That changed last summer when I saw a booger run across the yard. I was out burning some brush. I heard the neighbors' dogs barking. Typically, they're in their kennel, but they were barking like crazy over something. They bark at deer, but usually don't bark at things like raccoons or anything else that runs on the property.

I heard something running through the brush and thought, *"Cool! I'm going to see a deer."*

We don't see a lot of deer here, but we do see some monster sized ones. When we do see them, we consider it a treat.

I started watching the field between our house and our neighbor's house when I saw something that looked like it was sneaking around their house. It was on two legs.

Immediately I thought, *"It's a prowler."*

I had a big enough brush pile fire that I wasn't comfortable to leave it unattended and go into the house to get a gun. I just stood there watching whoever it was lurking around the neighbors' property.

Then I saw them run out from the house and pause for a second or two. The neighbors have a dusk to dawn light in their yard and I could see enough detail to realize that it wasn't a person. I couldn't see a lot of details, but I could tell that this creature was covered in hair. I couldn't tell from that distance if it was dark brown or black. It was backlit from the light.

I don't know if it saw me or not. To myself I said, *"Oh my gosh! It's a booger!"*

It took two steps, started to run, then paused again. It took a couple of giant steps and was over the hill. I heard a huge splash and thought it must have gone into the creek. I assume it jumped into the creek.

My husband came across the yard from their house. I still couldn't leave the fire. When he got close to me I told him, "You need to go get a gun!"

He knows I'm not scared of anything. I could go outside, lay down in the yard and sleep all night in a sleeping bag and not think twice about it. I'm not afraid of dogs. I'm not afraid of spiders. Really, I'm not afraid of much of anything. The only thing that scares me is snakes. So, he knew I wasn't faking.

It was the first time I'd ever encountered a *'booger'*, that I remembered at that time. I was trying to logic through what I had seen.

A couple of years before, there had been a bear seen in the area and bear sign, but nothing since. Whatever I saw didn't move like a bear. I'm not massively outdoorsy, but I am outdoorsy enough. I am quite logical about things. I'm not the kind who would see something and jump to the conclusion, *"I just saw a wood booger!"*

I couldn't rationalize what I'd seen. It had some very human characteristics. One was the way the legs were formed. The legs looked human. It didn't have hocks, or dog type legs or anything like that. The legs were normal, human looking legs.

I was sitting there trying to convince myself that I hadn't seen what I knew I saw while my husband was inside getting a gun. In my mind I went through every possibility of what it could have been, including a prowler.

I'm scientifically minded. I've been to college. I'm a healthy skeptic. I try to find a rational explanation for everything. Not everything out of the ordinary turns out to be something. I'm that kind of person.

My husband came back out and we didn't hear anything else. It was over and done with. After that, we started having booger happenings all over the place. We saw it a lot more often after that first encounter on our property.

I became a 'believer' after I saw the first booger. I'm at that age of fifty-something where you just don't care what people think about you anymore.

If I had to guess how big that booger was, I'd say it was about the same height as my husband – maybe 6' or 6'1". I think it was a juvenile. It was hunched over a little while it was moving very quickly. I didn't feel threatened. I was fascinated, but also a little confused about not knowing exactly what it was.

For the next few days after my initial sighting, we began to hear this strange verbalization in the woods. It sounded like the 'Samurai chatter', except it wasn't a whole lot of words. It wasn't like a whole conversation.

Something else strange that began to happen was that whenever we'd been out in the car and come home, as soon as we got out of the car and shut the doors, we'd hear a tree knock – a very loud and distinct tree knock.

We also heard one word, "Da'ak." It almost sounded like two syllables, but not quite. So, we call the booger who lives here Da'ak, because that was the word he used.

Many years ago, a lady went through and recorded every single word she heard the bigfoots say audibly. She tried to correlate all of that to figure out what they were talking about. I went through all that material and could not find the word "da'ak" anywhere. I couldn't help wondering if that was his name, if that was the word he used to say hello, or what it meant.

Now, we just refer to him as Da'ak.

My neighbors talk about hearing something rattling their door handle one night. This started a couple of days after my sighting. Also, they would find their flower watering cans moved and thrown across the garden.

Lawn chairs in our front yard were turned over, turned upside down, and thrown into different parts of the yard.

We started to hear big things walking through the woods and grunts. All of these happened, or at least we started noticing them, after I had my first sighting.

I've now seen Da'ak on multiple occasions. The first time was in May 2019. After that, things died down. In June we came home and found a tree branch laying across the driveway. There had been no high winds, rainstorms, or anything like that to cause the branch to fall. It was green wood that had been twisted off a tree and thrown into our driveway.

My husband got out of the car to clear it so we could get to the house. It was too big to drag away and had to be broken up before it could be moved. It was bigger around than my husband's forearm. He's a blacksmith and has large forearms.

Every time my husband broke off a piece of the branch, we'd hear a wood knock from the forest or a grunt. He finally got the driveway clear and we went on to the house. When we got out of the car there were two clear tree knocks. This repeated a lot after this. It didn't matter if we came home at 2:00 in the afternoon or 9:00 at night. Whenever we came home, got out of the car, and closed our doors, we heard two tree knocks.

It almost seemed like he was trying to communicate with us. Maybe he was saying, "Hey! I'm in the area!" or maybe "Welcome home!" I don't know for sure what it meant, but it was very consistent.

A couple of days later in June there was a tree that had been pulled out of the ground completely, roots and all and was laying against the back of our house. Again, there had been no storm, high winds, rain, or any reason for the tree to fall or be pulled up by the roots. It was as if it had been gently laid against the back of our house.

The same week, I was getting ready to go to the grocery store around 2:00 in the afternoon. It was a sunny, clear day. I was waiting on my husband because he wanted to come with me and run some errands of his own. I was waiting for him in the truck.

Up the hill about 10-15 feet is a big sycamore tree. I saw something move beside of that tree. I'm used to watching for deer. If they have an ear twitch, a tail twitch, or move at all, I often see them by the slightest motion in the forest. I thought the movement that had caught my eye was a squirrel on the tree or a deer behind the tree.

I continued to watch to see what was there. Then it popped it head out, I was sitting there looking straight at a sasquatch. I assumed, maybe erroneously, that I was looking at Da'ak. He was simply staring at me.

He had a beautiful face, dark black, and long black hair. He was very human looking but had a flatter nose, bigger eyes, and a more pronounced brow than a human. His head was a little conical, but not much. He looked a little more like a great ape than a chimp with a more rounded head. He was absolutely stunning!

He just sat there and blinked at me. We sat there for maybe 30 seconds staring eye to eye at each other. Then he moved his head back out of sight, and I didn't see him again. He had only been about 15-20 feet away from me where I was sitting in the truck. Just like that, he was gone back into the cover of the trees and bushes and out of sight. I would not have seen him in the first place had he not moved and popped his head around the tree.

Boogers are kind of childlike in their behavior. At least this one is. I have had a scary encounter, too, but it was not with the one we call Da'ak. It seems like he may be a juvenile. He behaves similar a 15-year old kid, kind of playful and sweet. What we've experienced here with him has been very enjoyable. There has been nothing aggressive where he's concerned.

My next sighting happened when we had gone to a state park in eastern Kentucky. We have a group of friends who try to get together every year and do a camping trip. Two years ago, we had just gotten our dog Bjorn who is a a mastidane, part mastiff and part great dane. He was a 70-pound puppy at the time when we got him. We took him with us on our camping trip.

It was July. The very first night we went to a state park. We thought we saw things moving in the woods and heard movement, but it was one of those situations where you think, "Maybe… maybe not. Not a big deal."

We heard tree breaks and things, but there is so much natural noise that goes on the woods at any time. There are so many things that can imitate the sounds we hope to hear associated with bigfoot. We didn't put a whole lot of stock into what we were hearing.

In our camp, we had set up a potty tent for privacy's sake. One of the guys who was with us decided he would skip the potty tent, and as men do, decided to go mark his territory outside of camp. He was taking care of business when he noticed a tree limb moving. It wasn't a normal movement. It was being moved upward and downward. There was no wind.

He looked up at where the branch was moving, standing there in a very vulnerable position. Suddenly, this 7-8-foot creature stepped out from behind a tree. He watched it looking back at him and kind of walked backwards, keeping eye contact with it as far as he could.

He went to his tent and didn't say a word to anyone about what had just happened.

The next day we went over to the campsite that was right across the road from us, which was where our friend had gone to mark his territory. A couple of the ladies who were camping in that area were wandering around and found a tree that had been struck by lightning.

They said, "You've got to come see this! It's really cool!"

We were going up the trail with them and my puppy was doing everything he could to discourage me and block me off the trail. He did not want me to continue going in that direction up the trail. He would get in front of my knees and block me. He was whimpering and carrying on. He was a big puppy at the time, but something clearly was upsetting him.

We went on up the trail to a tree that was not only broken but was twisted and laid over. I took pictures. A fresh break had been twisted around when it was broken like somebody had deliberately twisted it. There had been no wind or storms.

So, we got a little excited, thinking, *"Is there a bigfoot in the area?"*

We started looking around. There was a rock pile – rocks stacked on top of each other that hadn't been there the day before – beside this tree. We were all trying to logic it away.

"Maybe there were some kids here playing who decided to make a rock pile."

Then we found a print. It wasn't huge but was from someone who had their shoes off. It wasn't a regular human footprint but was oddly shaped. It looked like one we had found at my ~~girl~~friend's house.

On that path we had friends who went on up the hill. They told us they had found three more trees that were twisted and broken, pointing in the same direction as the one at the bottom of the path. These are not people who would have made up such a thing to try to sensationalize the situation or try to embellish a story, or make it seem scarier. They wouldn't do that.

Since I have a disability, on that day I couldn't continue the path to climb that hill. I have fibromyalgia that had flared up. Climbing was not an option that day.

We let it go and went back to our campsite. Later that afternoon we were playing cornhole (bag toss). One of my girlfriends was killing us. Every bag she threw went straight in the hole. She was wiping the floor with all of us.

Suddenly she grabbed her head and said, "What is that? What's making that noise? It hurts!"

From that point on, her 99% accuracy was gone. She was missing every bean bag toss, sometimes not even hitting the board.

I'm thinking, *"What's going on with her? Is she having a migraine? Is she having a stroke?"* Because of my health care experience, I was looking at her face, checking her pupils, and trying to evaluate whether she was having a serious issue.

Another guy with us had been an EMT. He was assessing her as well. We were trying to figure out if she was having a stroke and if we needed to get her to the hospital.

We went over and got her seated. All the pressure she was feeling and all the noise she was hearing was on the right side of her head. Then these sensations moved to the back of her head, which by this time was in the direction that the right side of her head had been facing at first.

She grabbed the back of her head and said, "What in the world is that? What is that noise? It hurts so bad!"

She told us it sounded like something was screaming in her head. She got up and turned to look in the direction where she thought the noise was coming from. The pressure moved to the left side of her head.

We finally realized she was not behaving like someone who was having a stroke. We started discussing the possibility of "infrasound." We assumed that maybe that was what had happened to her, but we had no proof. It's not like we had an infrasound meter with us to see if we were getting subsonic frequencies or whatever.

That was the beginning of things ramping up on that camping trip.

My husband and I are both of native decent. He went over to another campsite to make a tobacco offering. He thought, *"If I do this, if I make a tobacco offering, maybe everything will be good."*

I didn't know where he'd gone. I thought maybe he'd gone down to the bath house or something. My mastidane was going nuts. He was barking, whimpering, whining, and trying to hide under my chair all at the same time. He did not want "dad" to go over to the campsite across the road from us.

When he came back, Bjorn just leaned on him, sat there, and whimpered, obviously glad dad was back. He had been back maybe 20 minutes when we heard a tree fall. I heard a 100-year oak fall on our property a few years prior to this. It sounded like an explosion. When this tree fell, it sounded like it was a whole tree.

No. Apparently my husband's idea and tobacco offering were not good either.

That evening we heard vocalizations, knocking, Samurai speech, and the whole nine yards. We did not venture outside of our campsite that night.

The next day with the sunup, as crazy people will do, we decided to go back over to the other campsite. By that time, my cell phone had died. Nobody else had one with them either.

We found an adult sized sasquatch footprint, and with it a tiny, 3 or 4-inch print inside of the adult's footprint. I am so bummed that we didn't get a picture of it. The whole time we were there looking at it, my puppy was jerking on the leash, whining, and trying to get us to leave. He was acting like, *"Come on! Let's get out of here! I don't want to be here. This is bad!"* He was a nervous wreck as long as we were over on the other campsite.

We didn't see a sasquatch, but we had experienced so many things that seemed squatchy. There were many things that led us to believe it was a booger. We had no empirical proof of anything except the footprints we had found.

After we got home, I was talking to one of my buddies who has a radio show. I told him I felt like a squatch magnet after all the things I'd been through. That's my new nickname. *Squatch Magnet.*

My husband went to take the garbage out and there was a black squatch standing in the middle of the driveway. This creature he estimated to be 9-10 feet tall. It was monstrously huge. He kind of backed up and came back in the house.

It's not like that thing couldn't have ripped through the door and gotten into the house if it wanted. He said this one was extremely ape-like. Its hair was black and grey at the tips. He said that one way the creature stood, he looked entirely black. Then another way with a different angle of light, it looked very gray-haired.

I had a thought and called some knowledgeable bigfoot people to ask a question. *"Can these things track you? Would they?"*

We live about 10 miles away from the spot where we had been camping. The road is extremely winding and curvy.

The next night after his sighting in the driveway, I took the dog out. It was around 8:00 p.m. when I took Bjorn out to do his business. He started shaking and sniffing the air. He has a phenomenal nose on him.

He has what's called a 'choke collar' which is a self-correcting training collar. He started pulling on his leash so hard I knew it had to be hurting him to pull that hard against the leash. I started walking with him and he literally started herding me up to the porch and was trying to get me to go back inside.

The neighbor's dogs started acting up. They were going nuts. Then I heard a long whoop. It was very loud. It rumbled in my chest – loud, deep, moaning sound, like one of the Ohio whoops or the Sierra sound kind of thing. It almost sounded like a bray or a howl kind of sound.

I was on the path going back up onto the porch and I saw movement. There was a dark hairy thing coming at me that I would estimate to have been between 9-10 feet tall. It was running straight at me.

At this point, Bjorn was screaming and pulling hard on his leash. I was stunned, standing there with my mouth open, saying to myself, *"Holy crap!"* I couldn't move!

It ran at me and when it got close enough, one of our outdoor sensor lights came on. When the light cut on it turned right between where we park our car and a storage building. It went up the hill and was gone.

I got a bluff charge from this thing. It had the same kind of smell that we had picked up on while we were camping. The same kind of uneasy feeling was with me like we had experienced in the campsite. I don't know if was the same one or not, but it scared the daylights out of me!

After that, our puppy didn't want to go outside at all. It totally freaked him out. It was a good two weeks before he was comfortable going outside without me or my husband with him.

My neighbors also have a mountain cur. These dogs are bred to fight bear and wild boar. They're not afraid of anything. Their mountain cur would not go outside after dark by himself after this incident we had. They usually put him out the back door into a little fenced in area where he can go out and do what he needs to do. He wouldn't go out alone for that same two-week period that our dog wouldn't go out without us.

I was really, really sick after this sasquatch bluff charged me. I was extremely nauseated. I don't know if I got hit with infrasound or what. I was headachy and felt awful, like I'd been hit by a truck. It was crazy how sick I felt after that encounter. Just a few second with that creature seemed to shatter me.

I decided. *"Okay. I don't like these things. I don't like sasquatch. I don't want any more boogers around. I don't want to see any more boogers!"*

It didn't end there. There were four more encounters to come.

After being in health care, HR, and record keeping, I document everything that happens very, very well. I was trained to do that.

When I talked to my friend who is a member of the bigfoot arena of people devoted to the study of these creatures, he suggested we put up more motion sensor lights around the house, game cameras, and things of that nature. We did these things he suggested. We also bought more powerful headlamps, flashlights, and so on. When we do go out, we hope the increased lighting ability will either deter something from messing with us or we can at least see a lot better.

A couple of weeks after the bluff charge event, we were coming home when we saw a large rust colored sasquatch walking through a field up a hill and down a hill away from our house. We refer to this sasquatch as "Red." I don't know why, but I assumed this one was female. I call this creature 'her'.

She had to be at least 7 feet tall. The weeds in that field – iron weed, Joe Pye weeds and things like that are 5 or 6 feet tall when they're fully mature. I could see her head and shoulders above those tallest plants. This was the only time I ever saw her. She had a very pronounced cone shaped head. She was the third individual sasquatch I had seen.

We'd been out one day in the first part of August and got home around midnight. My husband thought he saw something with reddish-brown hair about 20-25 yards away. We were wondering if it was Red. We saw eyeshine and stuff. It didn't look like a deer. He hadn't seen her the first time I saw her, and I didn't see her that time.

Toward the end of August, I had to do some work on my truck. I was out in the driveway replacing a dashboard in the truck. It was about 3:00 in the afternoon. I heard the normal bipedal walking in the woods like what we hear around here a lot.

Then I heard something hit the truck. Then I heard something else hit the truck. Next, something hit the hood. I watched a rock skitter across the top of the hood. They were pebbles, not big rocks.

Something was trying to get my attention, not scare or harm me, but playfully let me know I was not alone. I looked around and didn't see anything.

I heard a whoop. It was high pitched whoop. Nothing else happened and I finished fixing the truck.

The next night my husband saw another, different sasquatch. It was a new one. It was completely gray, not black with a gray tinge like the other one. It was completely gray and about 8-9 foot tall. He only saw it for a moment.

We were grilling steaks that evening. The way our house is situated on a hillside, our porch sits about 8 feet off the ground. My husband was sitting inside the house, looking out through the door, and keeping an eye on the grill and the steaks. Suddenly the gray sasquatch's head appeared, looking over the edge of our porch up at the steaks. Then it looked at him, made eye contact, and ran off.

We went out and looked for tracks in that spot but didn't find anything. That was a cool experience for him.

Everything died down until October. We had tree breaks and rocks thrown at our outbuilding. About the middle of the month, we were getting ready to head to where my husband was working. I looked up on the hill and saw a dark sasquatch standing there. I slowed down for a minute to make sure I was seeing what I thought I was seeing.

The sasquatch was standing there between the trees straight out in the open. It wasn't hiding between trees. It wasn't hiding behind brush. It certainly wasn't me pretending, *"Oh! There's something dark there. It must be a squatch."* It was standing between some trees, but right out in the open.

I went on because I was running late, and this sasquatch paced our car. It ran parallel to our car about 30-35 yards up the ridge from us until I got to a curve, then I didn't see it anymore. It had stayed with us for a mile or mile and a half. I was driving about 20-25 miles an hour on that road, and it was pacing us the whole time. Then he dropped back.

Things were quiet again for a bit, but we started noticing a certain smell like garbage around the end of October. Whenever Da'ak is around, we don't get a lot of smell with him. Sometimes there is a bit of a wet dog smell with Da'ak, but we don't ever smell the nasty smells when he's around.

Bjorn had started being fearful again about going outside. We had to take him out. We'd hear weird noises in the woods, but nothing definitive that we could said it was a booger.

In November everything died down completely. It was if nothing had ever happened at all.

In December we heard some strange vocalizations and weird noises in the woods. There was a screaming sound that would almost go into a whistle. Another vocalization sounded like what the West Virginians would call a "ya-hooo." There would also come a response with another ya-hooo sound.

There were tree knocks as if they were communicating with each other. Then we started hearing something smack the side of the house. That was creepy. We don't know if that was a sasquatch or what.

Our game cameras picked up some really funky pictures starting in April of 2020. Our game camera was turned upside down. The game camera caught something large and hairy.

I got a picture of a sasquatch from our game camera on the hill. It's just lucky I saw him standing among the foliage. I blew the photo up and it's definitely a sasquatch. It looks exactly like the one we call Da'ak.

At that point I hadn't realized that the game cameras could do more than snapshots. I didn't know they could do video. When I found out we could do video, I set the game camera for this option and found it, once again, shaken and turned upside down.

The next time I saw a squatch was in the Daniel Boone National Forest. There were ten of us together who had gone for a camp out. The first day, a tree branch hit our cooler right in front of me. In the moment, I didn't think too much about it, thinking the branch had simply fallen from a tree.

On day two, my husband had gone to take a shower. He came back and heard something paralleling him in the woods. My husband is an outdoorsman. He grew up in the woods all his life. He grew up in a long rifle hunting community. He knows the woods. As a child he would run the woods from the time he got up in the morning until after dark.

Some folks had to leave after a couple of days due to work and other obligations. That left us with five people in camp.

We were sitting there and one of my girlfriends (an intelligent, college educated lady in her 50s) thought she saw a juvenile booger run through the woods. She didn't say anything at the time, arguing within herself, *"Maybe I did. Maybe I didn't"* kind of thing.

Around 1:00 a.m. that same night, all of us in three different tents were hearing stuff. We heard walking in woods, scratching on the tent. One girlfriend was brave enough to look out and saw some raccoons. She thought they were what had been scratching on the tent.

The ground where we were camping in the Daniel Boone National Forest was very hard. It literally took a hammer to pound the tent stakes into the ground and a claw hammer to pull the stakes out. When the friend who had heard the scratching on her tent started packing up and taking her tent down, she found one of her stakes pulled up out of the ground and lying beside of her tent. It would've taken massive strength to accomplish that without tools.

Another lady in a tent across from ours heard breathing outside her tent. She said it sounded like chuffing. The Daniel Boone National Forest is known for having a lot of black bears. The people who monitored the camp site where we were staying, clean up the trash and stuff like that said there had been no black bear sightings all summer in that campground. That didn't explain the breathing/chuffing she had heard.

The next morning ,we were all sitting around drinking our coffee, tea, and soda. One girlfriend said, "This is what happened to us last night…" and she told her story.

Then someone else said, "Well, this is what happened to me last night…"

Then one of them said she thought she had seen a booger run through the woods. Me, reacting and doing the dumbest thing anybody could do at that point decided to give a 'whoop'.

We were goofing off, laughing about it and stuff. Later that afternoon another tree branch hit the garbage cans where we were. We told the men who collected trash that they needed to do something about all the branches falling from the trees.

Later that evening, the same friend who developed the nausea and headache on one of our former camping trips said, "Oh, no! I'm having the same sensation of something screaming in my head again." She pointed like, "It's coming from over there!"

I pointed my binoculars in that direction and saw what looked like lichen on a tree – until it blinked then it just seemed to not be there. I panned back and forth and saw nothing.

I continued to try to find the face in the forest. I finally did and watched. It blinked occasionally, then he was gone. Don't ask me why, but I decided it would be a good idea to go for a walk in that direction but didn't go far. I turned around after a bit and went back to camp.

By about 9:00 it was completely dark. We had lighted some tiki torches and some table lamps going. We didn't build a big fire because it was hot enough. We saw movement in the woods near us. Then we started seeing eyeshine from two pairs of eyes. It was amber/golden.

We were panning again with our powerful flashlights. I was having trouble looking through the binoculars because it was steamy that night, too.

Suddenly there was something furry right behind one of my friend's tents. We hit it with our flashlights, and it took off running to the left.

It was the little one. It was 4 or 5 feet tall, very small. (*Note – you can add if you want. The whole sighting/interaction that night was about 15 -20 minutes total*)

Nothing else happened that night.

On the last morning we were getting ready to leave. We got everything packed up but weren't wanting to leave. So, we were sitting around talking, drinking sodas, teas, and having some snacks.

I looked up and that little sasquatch was right there in the open! It ran down the road, down a little hill out from our camp and down to the fishing dock. It ran down the little gravel road, wide out in the open. I happened to be the only one facing it. I wished someone else had seen it and not just me.

At that point we said, "Okay. Got to go. We've got to check out or they'll charge us for another day. We've got to get out of here."

I wanted to go follow the little guy and see what was going on. Then I decided, "No, you'd better leave the little one alone. Mom and dad might get mad!"

Our experience in the Daniel Boone National Forest was wonderful. We are planning our next group campout there again.

In July 2020, an odd thing happened with our sensor lights. As stated before, we put up several motion sensors on our property. We have two on the back of our house. On one occasion, my husband found one of the lights turned completely around to face the house. The light is about 9-10 feet off the ground and the screw is quite tight, so something like a raccoon would not have been able to turn it around *(see photo)*. When he climbed the ladder to turn it back around to face the back yard, he had to loosen the screw. The back of our house sits up against the wood line as a point of reference.

In August, my husband was out doing yardwork. He stopped for a moment when he heard a tree break on the hill behind our house. That night, around 10:30 p.m., Bjorn started barking toward the living room window. When we shined a flashlight out the window, we saw a booger face briefly staring back at us. It was dark haired, and around 8-9 ft tall.

After midnight of that same night, there was a "pecking" or "tapping" sound on the back or the house. Then around 1:15 a.m., something hit the back of the house very hard. Our motion sensor lights did not come on (which we discovered later was because they had been turned sideways). At 1:57 am, something hit the back of the house again. And again, at 2:05 a.m.

We didn't shine lights out the window when this was going on. But I didn't sleep that night either. And Bjorn's outside habits changed for several days. He is well trained and has his "place" in the yard, rarely going outside of it. But after the smacking noises, he started marking his territory around the front stairs and pathway between our house and where we park. That behavior, however, stopped after about a week.

Another sighting was had by my husband about a week later. All he could see was something tall and hairy inside the tree line up the hill a little way. That night, however, around 1:00 a.m., I heard something on the roof of the house, which I am the first to admit, may have just been my imagination.

About a week later, we went down to the creek near our home. Something was watching us, however. We caught glimpses of something dark and hairy a few times. At this point, we are used to seeing them and just don't worry about it, except when it's tapping or smacking on the house. But we've heard stories and had sightings of other things on the property, so we can't say whether the smacking and tapping is our booger or not.

We also have a driveway alarm. Bjorn now weighs over 100 pounds. He sounds very menacing when he barks to alert us that anyone is approaching or warn us that something that concerns him. The driveway alarm was installed so if he is out on his lead and we have a delivery person pull in the driveway, we can go get Bjorn quickly.

The driveway alarm went off about 3:00 a.m. on several nights, along with the motion sensors lighting up the property. These are events we've grown used to.

In September, my husband was cutting some brush behind the house along the tree line. Something caught his attention and he looked up the hill. About 15 feet away from him, there was a booger with short grey hair standing behind some bushes. He said it was not one he had seen before. By the time he came to get me, and we got to the back of the house, it was gone.

About 30 minutes later, my husband took some trash out, and saw the grey booger again. It paralleled him down the driveway as he took the trash to the curb, then just faded into the woods. That night, we heard a loud whoop.

A few days later, friends came to visit. My husband and my friend's husband were outside talking when they heard two distinct tree knocks, then a pause of about 30 seconds, then two more tree knocks.

About a week later, my husband and I were fighting. To clarify, we are members of a medieval society and "fights" in armor with rattan swords, which is the only way we ever fight. When the rattan, a type of solid bamboo, hits together, it sort of sounds like a tree knock. We hit swords a few times, then we got a response from the woods. I then hit his sword three times and we got three knocks back. I would hit two times, and we would get two knocks back. These were not echoing, they were responses. We then saw a flash of dark hair between some trees.

My cat-like curiosity is going to get me in trouble one of these days, like when I decided to "whoop" at camp. But I walked over to the edge of our driveway and there, sitting about 20-30 yards up the hill from me was a booger.

I said, "Hey buddy," in a calm voice.

I did not get a response. The booger, which I could see clearly, did not move, other than blink at me. I waved at him and would like to think it was Da'ak. I slowly backed away, not feeling threatened or scared, although not sure that I was being silly for not being afraid. I saw him blink again.

I did not see him stand up, and lost sight of him. We then heard him walk up the hill. We heard a tree break shortly after that.

Later that day, my husband was behind the house and he saw the booger again standing among the trees. He was about five yards away.

Sometimes when I have whistled for Bjorn, I will hear a whistle that sounds exactly like mine come from up the hill.

Earlier tonight, we had a booger staring in the window at us. When my husband shined a light out the window for a better look, it retreated into the woods.

It seems quite strange to me that all these sightings have occurred over the past two years. I try to consider every possibility that it could be anything but a sasquatch. I know that some of the knocks and noises are probably just me thinking it's my local booger, but the sightings have been very real and very consistent.

If this were someone else's story and I was reading it or hearing it, I probably wouldn't believe them. It's too much. Too convenient. Too fantastical to be believable. But it's made me think. I never didn't believe in boogers and I've come to understand why.

When I was around ten years old, I experienced my first booger sighting. I didn't remember until all of this began happening. I lived in West Virginia at the time and a big hairy creature would come to my window and peek in. I can't recall how many times or much about it, other that it was dark haired and very tall. I have vague memories of "talking" to it.

As we age, some of our memories are more like whisps of dreams, so I will never really know for certain. I just know that it seems like boogers have been a part of my life for a long time. I, in all my logic and reason, decided to ignore what was probably many times right in front of me.

They fascinate me. They have scared me. They have warmed my heart with their, what I will call, friendship.

I do not habituate. I do not go into the woods to "find" them or look for tracks or hair. It is their place. If I do happen upon a track, it will only serve to help me know it is not just imagination or my eyes playing tricks on me.

Although I know these things aren't born from my imagination, the healthy skeptic within me always asks questions to ensure that what I know I see - is what I actually see.

Camping Trip in the Daniel Boone National Forest
October 18-25, 2020

My group of six friends returned to the Daniel Boone National forest for a much-needed week of camping. My mastadane, Bjorn, immediately started acting out of character. He whimpered a lot starting on day one. He was unusually aggressive and nervous all week.

We were better prepared this time, given our last experiences in this location, bringing our cameras, fleer, and other equipment. We did not get any evidence on the equipment, however. Our batteries drained very quickly all week.

Night 1 – Sunday, October 18th

My husband heard strange noises all night on this first night. Something slapped the tent at least two or three times I heard a couple more tent slaps after he went to sleep. We heard lots of walking around near our tent, but the ground was very hard packed and not conducive to any type of tracks.

On the dock down the hill, we heard rocks clacking. We also heard a single tree knock. There were a lot of geese and crows that called all night long. My husband heard something that sounded like a very large rock being dropped in the lake, producing a very loud splash. There were weird scream sounds that could have been a bobcat or a screech owl. We also heard several whoops.

There was something that sounded like an owl, but there was not the usual trill at the end. I also heard a howl. My husband heard a young female voice that sounded like she said "zipper" right outside the tent. Activity lasted from about 8:30 p.m. until about 6 a.m. on and off.

My friend Joy heard rustling in the woods several times during the night. She said it sounded like possible bi-pedal walking.

Night 2 – Monday, October 19th

Joy was hit with infrasound and had a horrible headache. The headache woke her up on and off all night.

My husband heard walking around throughout the night. He heard something playing with the chain on the tiki torch topper. He had gone to the bathhouse at one point earlier in the night and when he came out there was a large bi-pedal creature about 8-foot tall standing about 30 yards away. It was too dark to get a lot of detail. He got hit with infrasound and was really nauseated when he got back to camp. He heard a tree break during his walk back from the bathhouse.

He also saw the silhouette of a possible juvenile sasquatch go through the woods and black out the light from the ranger's house while we were sitting around the fire. While we continued sitting there, all of us heard several tree knocks and a few whoops.

I had seen a juvenile during the daytime earlier that day run through the woods.

That night I saw a silhouette in between the tiki torch and tent. I thought the torch had gone out. Then I saw a large unidentified creature move away. I didn't look outside at the time. I couldn't get to the window with the way we had stuff set around in the tent. This was followed by a I heard a growl behind the tent.

Night 3 – Tuesday, October 20th – MAJOR EVENTS ON THIS DAY

About 1:00 a.m., I heard lots of sounds, knocks, and bi-pedal walking around the tent. Something slapped the back of the tent then the side of the tent.

Things died down a little, so I tried to go to sleep. I was awakened by bi-pedal walking in front of the tent. I saw a large silhouette in front of the tent. It was standing in front of the door between the tiki torch and the tent. It took its finger and raked down the tent making a loud sound like nails scratching on the nylon tent. I could clearly see the finger pushing in the fabric of the tent door.

It ran around to its left to the back of the tent, then came to the left side of the tent and slapped it. The tent is cross shaped. It then went to the window which was shut and pressed its face against the window. I could see the nose and brow ridge.

It turned its head (still pressed against the tent) toward the sound I made as I quietly tried to get up. I got my night vision goggles and opened the window but did not see anything. There were several grunts and bipedal walking. In the distance, I heard an extremely large tree break.

I was unable to go back to sleep. I was so nervous, that I grabbed my .38 pistol which I knew I wouldn't use because it would just make things worse. If it were the juvenile sasquatch outside snooping about, I wouldn't shoot it because I wouldn't want mom or dad to come tear my arms off.

I went outside to look around mostly because it was creepier to be in the tent and unable to see than outside in the dark. I sat down alone to record and listen. Right before I hit record, I heard a stick about a foot long, whiz past my head and hit the picnic table in front of me. The whizzing sound was like when you take a stick and throw it side arm and it rotates in the air. Afterwards, I heard what sounded like a big "plop" in the lake like what it would sound like it someone cannonballed into the water.

I hollered at my friends, "There's major stuff going on out here!"

Joy and Bea joined me outside. My husband, Joy's husband Chad, and our friend Mike were still sound asleep.

Bea stated she had heard lots of tree knocks and bangs. She had a harder slap on the tent than the previous night. There was lots of crunching near the tent in the gravel.

Joy thought she heard raccoons in her area. But before that, she heard a small stick hit the tent. It was approximately around the same time the stick got thrown at me when we talked about it. She heard rustling around the tent. She felt the same nervousness and did not look out her window. Joy stated her husband heard the stick hit the tent but just rolled over and went back to sleep.

As we were sitting outside, we heard 3 very distant and distinct whoops.

Night 3 –Wednesday, October 21 – Squatch Hunting Night

Wednesday during the day, we walked around the point to the other little inlet near out came down by the water's edge. We found two small squatch prints slightly larger than my foot. They were fresh. I got a photo of one but forgot to get a photo of the second.

We traveled a short distance up the road to do some recording and see if we could connect with a squatch. Joy and my husband got hit with infrasound. We heard a few whoops and whistles. Joy got very light-headed and nauseous. She saw a squatch sitting and leaned against a tree. It changed positions to a more upright one. She lost sight of it.

Night 4 – Thursday October 22

My husband and I drove to the store. When we got back to camp no one was at camp. Several had gone out to run errands as well. My husband saw a juvenile squatch run across the camp.

Later that night, I was sound asleep, and my husband heard a lot of walking around and then a popping noise like when someone pulls a cork out of a bottle. He woke me up to tell me about it. There was a very loud tree knock. Then he fell asleep. I heard tree knocks that seemed to be going back and forth between one coming from behind the tent and one on a point over the inlet on the lake where we were camped. There were two tree knocks and two in response, single knock, single response. This went on for about 30 minutes.

Night 5 – Friday, October 23rd

Bea had gone to the privy tent. The manager's office is right up against the back of our camp area. All the outside lights were on, which was very weird. Bea has camped in this same spot for over ten years and said it was very odd for the place to be so well lit after hours. She looked up toward the lights.

She saw a silhouette of a sasquatch which was very tall and had a conical shaped head. She said it took two steps then completely disappeared into the darkness. It was her first sighting of a squatch, and she was so excited. She said she didn't feel fear. She heard a little walking around that same night, but it wasn't as much as on Tuesday night.

Night 6 – Saturday, October 24th

There were five or six tree knocks, and a weird metallic clanging. There was a loud huff outside our tent window. I looked up to see something blocking the tiki torch, then it moved away. I opened the tent window, but it was already gone.

Later, something came back to the side of the tent and urinated. I could see a silhouette backlit by the tiki torch and heard the sasquatch relieving itself, or marking territory, which seemed to go on forever. There was a horrible smell. It rained after that, so the smell was gone the next morning.

I'm not sure why I have had the good and bad fortune, depending on your point of view, of having so many encounters with boogers. It seems like once I saw the one last year, the flood gates opened to a whole new world for me. If I were listening to someone tell this many encounters, I would be very skeptical of them. However, even my concern that I've lost my sanity is allayed by the fact that my husband and two of my very best friends, all of which are intelligent, rational people, have experienced many of the same sightings, sounds, and anomalies right along with me.

Even with the couple of "nervous" encounters that I've had, I really want to see more. I want to learn more about these marvelous and elusive creatures.

Historical Accounts of Bigfoot Sightings
From public domain information and oral tradition

The earliest documented sighting of a huge hairy humanoid creature on the east coast go back to the year 986 when the well-known Viking explorer, Leif Ericson first set foot on the American continent.

Ericson's adventures brought him to the east coast of North America along with a crew of Viking explorer warriors. One of these men recorded an incident on their first landing in which they encountered manlike beasts.

For anyone who has studied the characteristics of the ancient Vikings, it is undeniably ironic that they described these beasts as "horribly ugly, hairy, swarthy, and with great black eyes." Those of other civilizations who encountered the Vikings may have described them in much the same way.

What could possibly have impressed these notable warrior explorers to leave the company of these creatures?

Leif Ericson told of seeing huge hairy men who towered over him and his men. These men dwelled in the woods, had a very foul odor, and a deafening shriek.

Public Domain Image – The Landing of the Vikings by Arthur C. Michael (1919)

According the Viking accounts of this leg of their exploration, they had several encounters with the huge hairy men.

They gave the name Skellring to the creatures. It was a Norse term that was not very flattering.

Basically, the barbarian Norsemen were calling these creatures barbarians. Apparently, they were bigger, hairier, and more foul smelling than Leif Ericson and his men.

Did Daniel Boone Really Kill a Bigfoot?
Public Domain Information and Oral Tradition

According to oral tradition, Daniel Boone came into the Kentucky territory on several long rifle hunting expeditions in the 1700s. On one of these forays into Kentucky, he encountered and killed a ten-foot tall, muscular, hair-covered man. He called the creature a "Yea-hoo" or "Yahoo."

The incident was recorded in is diaries and it is said that he told the story on many occasions in his life-time and especially in his older years a true incident.

Public Domain Image of Daniel Boone
Alonzo Chappell, 1851

Historical Records of Bigfoot Sighting on the West Coast Go Back to 1774

In 1792, Jose Mariano Mozino wrote in his journal about incidents that happened while he and his crew were exploring the Pacific Coast. This expedition was sponsored by both the Spanish and the English.

Mozino's journal was named *Noticias de Nutka: An Account of Nootka Sound in 1792.* The journal did not come to light until 1913 and had to be translated to English. It was written as the exploration of the Pacific coast was in progress. Of the interesting things he recorded in this journal, there are references that can easily be believed that he was referring to a bipedal hairy creature unlike the indigenous people of the west coast.

The viceroy of Spain, Juan Vincente Guemes, instructed the explorers to chronicle the events of their journey and to record as much as possible about the people living in the region. It was under these instructions that Jose Mariano Mozino recorded with detail the progress, discoveries, and encounters of the expedition. **The journal now resides in the** <u>**Beinecke Rare Book and Library Collection**</u>.

One group of indigenous people they interacted with were known as the Nootka tribe. He also refers to a creature known by the natives and referred to Matlog.

This creature lived in the mountains and was a source of great distress to the people in the area. Mozino describes this creature as one having a huge monstrous body covered in black bristly hair. He noted the head to be like a human's head in shape, only much larger.

He also recorded that the teeth of this creature were larger and sharper than human teeth and appeared similar to those of a bear or wolf. He observed that the creature's arms were long with curved claws on the fingers. He was told that the creature emitted a terrible scream.

The local natives believed the Matlog was a demon. There is no indication that he or the group of explorers had a personal encounter with the Matlog.

A huge gap in recorded accounts of this creature exists. In 1928 a trapper by the name of Muchalat Harry told an unbelievable story of his encounter with a similar creature.

He had been staying among the Nootka Indians but decided to go north up the Conuma River by canoe. At night, he made camp, planning to resume his trip the following morning. He settled in for the night by the campfire. One can only imagine his terror as he felt himself being lifted and carried away. According to Harry, he was carried between two and three miles away from his campsite.

Not only had he been carried so far by a creature of unbelievable strength, but he found himself deposited in a camp of Matlog in which he estimated were at least twenty individual creatures.

These Matlog were male and female, different ages, and different sizes according to Harry's account. He found himself in the middle of a Matlog colony. He was apparently a curiosity to them, and they all stared at him.

He didn't know if their intention was to eat him, keep him captive, or let him go eventually. When he spotted a pile of bones, the terror of the situation seized him.

The creatures appeared to be very interested in the blanket he was wrapped in. When they lost interest and busied themselves with normal activity (for them) as the day went on, Harry decided to make a run for it.

As unbelievable as it seems, it is reported that Harry ran forty-five miles without stopping, motivated by fear that the Matlog would recapture him and perhaps make a dinner of him. When he reached the Nootka village that he had left only a few days earlier, they took him back in. It is said that it took three weeks for him to recover from the ordeal and he never went back into the woods alone after that.

http://monstrumathenaeum.org/earliest-known-recorded-history-of-bigfoot-sightings-pacific-coast/

Sightings of the 1800s

In 1846, residents of Arkansas reported accounts of a wild man that scared many. It was reported that one of his footprints measured in at 22 inches.

In September of 1818, the Watchman Newspaper of New York State reported a creature encounter near Ellisburgh, New York. It was stated, "a gentleman of unquestionable veracity saw an animal resembled the Wild Man of the Woods."

This creature was described as a very large man covered in hair, which walked out of the woods a few yards in plain view of the witness. When the creature saw the man, it turned and ran away. It left extremely large human-like footprints.

In 1851, two hunters watched a large hairy man-like creature trying to catch a calf from a herd of cattle in Greene County, Arkansas. The hunters described the creature a being gigantic and with a likeness of humans. They stated the creature's body was "covered with hair and the head with long locks that fairly enveloped the neck and shoulders."

When the creature realized the hunters were nearby, it stopped chasing the calf and stared at the hunters momentarily before it ran into the woods, leaving behind large footprints.

Public Domain Image from 1870

Documented Sightings from the Early 1900s

1901 Man Monkey

"The Hunt for the Man-Monkey" was written by English essayist Percy Longhurst in 1901. It is written as non-fiction about a cryptozoological expedition said to have taken place in Borneo during the 1880s. The story by Longhurst is presented as an account of an actual event told to him by Captain Bywater who was the captain of a steam yacht. The yacht was owned by a wealthy man who wanted to take a group of friends for a cruise along some Malaysian island.

One of the travelers had heard stories about a large ape-like creature which was reported to live in the jungles. They decided they would try to capture one and take it to the London Zoo. They had no luck and went on to a place called Sarawak where they asked for permission from the Rajah to hunt the man monkey. The Rajah, Sir Charles Brooke decided to accompany them on the expedition.

"... they neared the locality wherein it was supposed was the home of the Mai-as. The Dyaks and Malays spread themselves out in advance of the party of Englishmen, beating the forest, and all the while keeping a sharp look-out for the dreaded man-monkey. All moved with the greatest caution, and the keen, anxious faces of the natives showed that they considered the business in hand to be no child's play.

Presently a loud shout from one of the Dyaks brought the party up all standing, and with their fingers on the triggers of their rifles (for there was no telling how the Mai-as might resent their intrusion) the Englishmen advanced to where the native had perceived the hideous animal standing at the foot of a tree.

Slowly the Mai-as began to climb the tree, in the lower boughs of which could be seen his house, constructed of thick branches cunningly interlaced.

Then began the trouble to induce him to descend, and if possible to drive him to the open country; for in the dense forest there was but small chance of surrounding him and taking him alive, as the Englishmen wished. Stones, clods of earth, and sticks were hurled at him, and then he leisurely descended. As his assailants hurriedly retired he reached the ground and disappeared along one of the forest paths.

In strength and bulk, although not in height, he is superior to the terrible black gorilla of Central Africa, while in appearance, at a short distance, he looks like a short and very broad native, being a brownish-black, and standing about 4 ft. high. In the face he is far less repulsive than his neighbour the orang-outang or the chimpanzee.

Hard at his heels came the hunters, until the Mai-as caught sight of a solitary palm tree not a mile away. Reaching it he climbed up, despite the slippery trunk and the absence of branches. About 30ft. above the ground the creature stopped, and, holding on by his arms and legs, watched his pursuers, who, having treed their game, were now engaged in discussing how to secure it.

It was suggested that the tree be cut down and the Mai-as secured as it fell, but no tools were at hand, and no one, moreover, felt at all inclined to risk a hand-to-hand encounter with the huge animal.

At last it was decided that the Mai-as be induced (if possible) to descend from the tree, and then, after breaking its leg with a bullet to disable it, to attempt to stun it by a blow on the head, and while insensible to bind it with strong ropes. It was by no means a satisfactory plan, but the Englishmen were anxious to secure the brute, if possible, alive. And no other method of doing so suggested itself.

This having been settled, the next move was to get the Mai-as down. There was nothing to throw at it and, according to the natives, its strength was so great that it would be able to remain in its present position for an incalculable period.

At length, tempted by a bribe of 200 pounds, a young Malay offered to climb the tree, and by irritating the animal induce it to descend.

The brave fellow first fixed on his hands and feet coverings of hide with strong thorns fixed therein to enable him to get a hold of the slippery bark, which offered no projections or footholds whatever; and taking with him a "shooting-iron," he resolutely began the ascent. This "shooting-iron" is really a blow-pipe, somewhat similar to that used by the Indians of the River Amazon, but having a sharp spear-head firmly fixed at one end in such a manner as not to interfere with the passage of a dart through the hollow pipe.

Breathlessly the onlookers watched the young man as, foot by foot, he crept up the tree, until when within about 8ft. of the Mai-as (who so far had showed no inclination to move) he raised his weapon and prodded the animal in the leg, whereupon the huge creature retreated higher up the tree. The Malay crept after him, and repeated his spear-thrust, and again the Mai-as retreated, while the daring hunter followed him.

Afraid that the tree would not bear his ponderous weight if he went any higher—it was already beginning to sway dangerously—the Mai-as stopped and, leaning down, stretched out one hand, and with a lightning-like movement grasped the iron spear - head.

Then he commenced to pull, and hand over hand, hanging on solely by his muscular legs, he commenced to haul up the wretched Malay, who was powerless, the blow-pipe being attached to his wrist by a strong leather thong.

Little by little the powerful brute drew up the man until, holding the blowpipe with one hand, he reached down with the other and wreathed his huge hand in the thick, luxuriant hair of the miserable native, who, paralyzed by fear, could do no more than gaze at the savage face of his captor with terror-stricken eyes.

Spell-bound with horror, the Englishmen below then saw the Mai-as with a single twist wrench the Malay from the tree and commence to swing his victim backwards and forwards by the hair, chuckling all the time with fiendish satisfaction.

Too fascinated with horror to use their rifles and slay the monster or else kill the man and put a merciful end to his sufferings, the hunters watched the wild man swinging the Malay faster and faster.

With an unearthly yell of devilish malignity, he hurled him down. The wretched man turned over and over as he fell and came to the ground with a heavy thud that sent a sickening thrill through the hearts of the watchers. They rushed to the spot, but it was too late—the man was stone dead.

Furious with rage one of the Englishmen raised his rifle and, hastily sighting, fired. The bullet struck the Mai-as fairly in the ribs under the left arm, and with a cry the brute slid to the ground, where for one- brief moment he supported himself against the tree, with one hand on the wound. Then with a groan, quite human in its intensity, he pitched forward on his face, dead.

It should be mentioned that the party, after the unsuccessful hunt related, relinquished the idea of securing a live specimen, and the dead body of the monkey having been skinned and the flesh removed, the skeleton was brought back to England, where it remains in the possession of the owner of the yacht who had organized the expedition."

"WRENCHED THE MALAY FROM THE TREE, AND COMMENCED TO SWING HIS VICTIM BACKWARDS AND FORWARDS BY THE HAIR."

In 1920

Geologist Francois De Loys led a party of individuals through the jungles of Venezuela in 1920 during the rush to find geologic evidence of oil deposits. The group was fighting the heat and exhaustion, so they decided to rest near a water source.

Two five-foot "screamers" approached the group, displaying ape-like behaviors. They shook tree branches, screamed in ape-like voices, and shook broken tree branches at the group, walking bipedally. They even threw their own feces at the men.

Reacting in fear and exhaustion, the two creatures were shot at by the group. The male escaped, but the female was killed. The male retreated into the jungle.

The creature's body was eventually propped up, sitting on a crate and its head supported by a stick. It was said to be five feet tall with no tail. It had thirty-two teeth. De Loys took the remains of the creature with the group as they moved on. It was lost, however, some time during the expedition. Only one photograph was taken of the creature.

Public Domain Image of De Loy's Ape – 1920

Wildmen

"The wild man (also wildman, or "wildman of the woods") is a mythical figure that appears in the artwork and literature of medieval Europe, comparable to the satyr or faun type in classical mythology and to *Silvanus*, the Roman god of the woodlands. The defining characteristic of the figure is its "wildness"; from the 12th century they were consistently depicted as being covered with hair." - Wikipedia

Creative Commons Attribution-ShareAlike License

Wildmen stories are found among the indigenous population of the Pacific Northwest. The legends existed prior to a single name for the creature. They differed in their details both regionally and between families in the same community. Similar stories of wildmen are found on every continent except Antarctica. Ecologist Robert Michael Pyle argues that most cultures have human-like giants in their folk history: "We have this need for some larger-than-life creature."

In 1951, Eric Shipton had photographed what he described as a Yeti footprint. This photograph generated considerable attention and the story of the Yeti entered popular consciousness. The notoriety of ape-men grew over the decade, culminating in 1958 when large footprints were found in Del Norte County, California by bulldozer operator Gerald Crew. Sets of large tracks appeared multiple times around a road-construction site in Bluff Creek. After not being taken seriously about what he was seeing, Crew brought in his friend, Bob Titmus, to cast the prints in plaster. The story was published in the Humboldt Times along with a photo of Crew holding one of the casts.

Locals had been calling the unseen track-maker "Big Foot" since the late summer, which Humboldt Times columnist Andrew Genzoli shortened to "Bigfoot" in his article. Bigfoot gained international attention when the story was picked up by the Associated Press. Following the death of Ray Wallace – a local logger – his family attributed the creation of the footprints to him. The wife of L.W. "Scoop" Beal, the editor of the Humboldt Standard, which later combined with the Humboldt Times, in which Genzoli's story had appeared, has stated that her husband was in on the hoax with Wallace.
1958 was a watershed year not just for the Bigfoot story itself but also for the culture that surrounds it. The first Bigfoot hunters appeared following the discovery of footprints at

Bluff Creek, California. Within a year, Tom Slick, who had funded searches for Yeti in the Himalayas earlier in the decade, organized searches for Bigfoot in the area around Bluff Creek.

As Bigfoot has become better known and a phenomenon in popular culture, sightings have spread throughout North America. In addition to the Pacific Northwest, the Great Lakes region and the Southeastern United States have had many reports of Bigfoot sightings

content is available under

Public Domain Image of Medieval Wildman

THE COURIER, CONNELLSVILLE, PA.,

FRIDAY OCTOBER 4, 1895.

A Big Scare at Sewickley.

For more than a year the people on Sewickley creek below West Newton have been troubled by some strange animal which carries off sheep, pigs and other animals from their farms. Until late no one ever saw the beast, and even those who have lately seen it cannot tell whether it is a catamount, wolf or panther. During the past week parties have been scouring the country in search of it. Late reports from the district say that the beast's lair has been found in a ledge along the creek, and all around are bones of its victims. A close watch is being kept on the lair and it is expected that the beast will soon be killed. It is a mystery as to how it got so far away from the mountains and as to what sort of an animal it is. Great excitement prevails in the neighborhood, and all keep close to their homes at night or travel heavily armed.

HAGERSTOWN, MD., FRIDAY, MAY 5, 1871.

THE TENNESSEE WILDMAN

The Jackson (Tenn.) *Whig* of the 13th instant says: "We learn that between Sobby and Crainsville, on what is called Piney, in McNairy county, a strange and frightful being has been observed for several weeks. He is said to be seven feet high, and possessed of great muscular power. His eyes are unusually large, and fiery red; his hair hangs in a tangled and matted mass of jet below his waist, and his beard reaches below his middle. His entire body is covered with hair, and his whole aspect is most frightful. He shuns the sight of men, but approaches with wild and horrid screams of delight every woman who is unaccompanied by a man. He sometimes, with great caution, approaches houses, and should he see a man he runs away with astonishing swiftness, leaping the tallest fences with the ease of a deer, defying alike the pursuit of men and dogs. He has frightened several women by attempting to carry them off, as well as by his horrid aspect, and the whole country around Sobby is in consternation. The citizens are now scouring the woods, and are determined either to capture of drive off the monster.

New York Times. 06 January 1894 Newark, N.J., Jan. 6. –

The Residents of the vicinity of Dover are excited over the sudden appearance of a wild man near the town.

He has taken up his abode in the vacant Mellon homestead, and first made his appearance to several women who were passing near the place. He uttered threatening sounds and started toward them, causing the women to run away.

A searching party was sent out, but the man could not be found. A few days later he was seen running wild through the woods, wearing no clothing. Another party was sent out, and dogs were used.

When the man was surrounded, he grabbed one of the dogs and killed it with a club, and then made his escape. He is still at large.

THE COMPILER.

Gettysburg, Monday, June 2, 1851.

Wild Man of the Woods.—A gigantic man of the woods has been discovered in Greene county, Arkansas, and a party has been organized to endeavor to catch him. When last seen he was pursuing a herd of cattle, who were flying in a state of great alarm, as if pursued by a dreaded enemy. On seeing the party who discovered him, he looked at them deliberately for a short time. turned, and ran away with great speed, leaping from twelve to fourteen feet at a time. His footprints measured thirteen inches each. He was of gigantic structure, the body being covered with hair, and the head with long locks that fairly enveloped his neck and shoulders.

Public Domain Image from 1894

The Long Island Star Newspaper Brooklyn New York. 16 September 1818. Wednesday. Page 3.

Sackets-Harbor, Sept. 8.

Report says, that in the vicinity of Ellisburgh was seen on the 30th ult- by a gentleman of unquestioned veracity, an animal resembling the *Yo-ho*, or *Wild man of the Woods*. It is stated that he came from the woods within a a few rods of this gentleman—that he stood and looked at him, then took his flight in a direction which gave a perfect view of him for some time. He is described as bending forward when running, hairy—and the heel of the foot narrow, spreading at the toes. Hundreds of persons have been in pursuit for several days ; but nothing further is heard, or seen of him

The frequent and positive manner in which this story comes, induces us to notice it. We wish not to impeach the veracity of this highly favored gentleman— yet, it is proper that such naturally improbable if not impossible events, should be established by the mouth, of at least, two or three eye-witnesses, to entitle them to credibility.

———

Weekly Arkansas Gazette. Little Rock, Arkansas. 30 May. 1851. Friday. Page 3.

A Wild Man of the Woods.—The Memphis Enquirer gives an account of a wild man recently discovered in Arkansas. It appears that during March last Mr. Hamilton, of Greene county, Ark., while hunting with an acquaintance, observed a drove of cattle in a state of apparent alarm, evidently pursued by some dreaded enemy. Halting for the purpose, they soon discovered, as the animals fled by them, that they were followed by an animal bearing the unmistakeable likeness of humanity. He was of gigantic stature, the body being covered with hair, and on the head was long locks that fairly enveloped his neck and shoulders. The "wild man," after looking at them deliberately for a short time turned and ran away with great speed, leaping from twelve to fourteen feet at a time. His footprints measured thirteen inches each.

This singular creature, the Enquirer says, has long been known, traditionally, in St. Francis, Greene, and Poinsett counties, Ark., sportsmen and hunters having described him seventeen years since. A planter indeed, saw him very recently, but withheld his information lest he should not be credited, until the account of Mr. Hamilton and his friend placed the existence of the animal beyond cavil.

A great deal of interest is felt in the matter, by the inhabitants of that region, and various conjectures have been ventured in regard to him. The most generally entertained idea appears to be that he was a survivor of the earthquake disaster which desolated that region in 1841. Thrown helpless upon the wilderness by that disaster, it is probable that he grew up in his savage state, until he now bears only the outward resemblance of humanity.

So well authenticated have now become the accounts of this creature, that an expedition is organizing in Memphis, by Col. David C. Cross and Dr. Sullivan, to scout for him.

Southern Shield. Helena, Arkansas. 01 May. 1852. Saturday. Page 3

THE WILD MAN AGAIN.—We are credibly informed by a gentleman of this city, that the " wild man " has been seen again in the swamps of Arkansas. He derived his information from two gentlemen, who were out hunting, and approached as near as twenty paces to him. His appearance was so frightful that they did not attempt to approach nearer. He is described by them as being about 7 feet 2 inches high, and covered completely with black hair, interspersed now and then with gray. The story or the representations of him as last seen, published in some of our papers, they pronounce untrue. He has no claws to his hands and feet, nor is he eight or nine feet high: still he would be a curiosity worth seeing. We understand it is the intention of some of our citizens to capture him if possible. In the way of shows, he would be the " wild mare, " with the " hippodrome " thrown in.

Memphis Express.

The Sentinel. Waterville, Maine. October 1886.

An affrighted Frenchman from over the line arrived in Elm City. The Frenchman's story, which is implicitly believed, is that three men were camping out in the woods about a hundred miles north of Moosehead Lake.

Two of the campers were away from the camp for a week and came back to find the dead body of their companion.

They went for help and reinforced by a dozen others searched the woods for the unknown murderer.

It proved to be a terrible wild man, ten feet tall, with arms seven feet in length, covered with long, brown hair. The party fired several shots at him and finally succeeded in reaching a fatal spot, laying the monster low.

Public Domain Image

WHAT IS IT ?

A STRANGE CREATURE CAP-TURED ABOVE YALE.

A British Columbia Gorilla.

(Correspondence of The Colonist).

YALE, B. C., July 3rd, 1882.

In the immediate vicinity of No. 4 tunnel, situated some twenty miles above this village, are bluffs of rock which have hitherto been unsurmountable, but on Monday morning last were successfully scaled by Mr. Onderdonk's employes on the regular train from Lytton. Assisted by Mr. Costerton, the British Columbia Express Company's messenger, and a number of gentlemen from Lytton and points east of that place who, after considerable trouble and perilous climbing, succeeded in capturing a creature which may truly be called half man and half beast. "Jacko," as the creature has been called by his capturers, is something of the gorilla type standing about four feet seven inches in height and weighing 127 pounds. He has

Public Domain - Medieval Carving of a Wild Man or Hairy Man between 1390 and 1400

Public Domain – Bronze Sculpture Paulus Vischer (c. 1498-1531): Wild Man